North Lakeland Walks with Children

Mary Welsh

Published by Sigma Leisure – an imprint of
Sigma Press, 5 Alton Road, Wilmslow, Cheshire SK9 5DY, England.

British Library Cataloguing in Publication Data
A CIP record for this book is available from the British Library.

ISBN: 1-85058-601-2

Typesetting and Design by: Sigma Press, Wilmslow, Cheshire.

Cover: 'family outing' – Keith Whitwell

Maps and illustrations: Christine Isherwood

Printed by: Interprint Ltd, Malta

Contents

Location

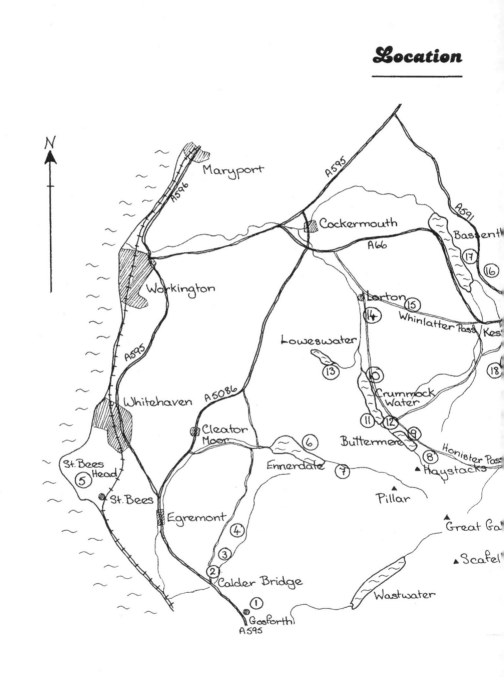

Map

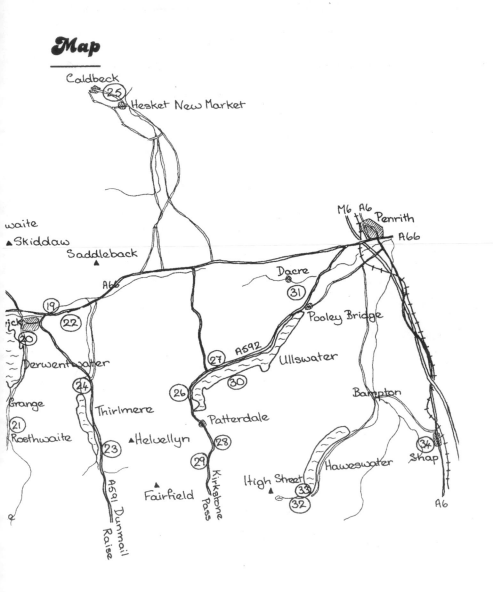

Caldbeck
25
Hesket New Market

M6 A6
Penrith
A66

waite
▲ Skiddaw
Saddleback ▲

A66

Dacre
31

19
ick
22
Pooley Bridge

20
A592
27
Ullswater
Derwentwater
30
24
26
Bampton
Grange
Thirlmere
Patterdale
21
▲ Helvellyn
28
Shap
Rosthwaite
23
34
29
Haweswater
Fairfield ▲
Kirkstone Pass
High Street
33
A591 Dunmail Raise
32
A6

Before you Begin

Introductory notes on the text

This is a very unusual book, intended to be read by both parents and children. The following conventions have been used to make the book as useful as possible to both categories:

1. **Directions are numbered (as in this example) and appear in bold test so that they can be seen at a glance.**

☺ Information for the children is set in a contrasting typestyle. This is to be read aloud, or for them to read themselves.

Other information for parents appears in bold text.

Questions (and answers) are in the same type style, with "**Q**" (and "**A**").

Sketch maps

The maps are intended only as a rough guide and are not drawn to scale. Unless otherwise stated, north is upwards. Only buildings important to the route are shown. Numbers refer to the directions given in the text.

Roads	=	a continuous, heavy, double line
Footpaths	=	a dashed line
Rivers	=	a continuous, light, double line
Streams	=	a continuous single line
Parking	=	P

1. Gosforth

Gosforth is a large delightful village. The name is thought to mean 'ford of geese'; as you leave the car park look for the cobbled plaque with the name of the village and a fine slate portrait of two geese set into it. The village is surrounded by pastures and beyond stand some of the highest mountains in England. It is possible that a church existed in this area in the 8th century. The hogback tombs and stone cross date from before 1066. It is not mentioned in the 1086 Domesday Book because at this date this area was part of Scotland. This pleasant, undemanding walk takes you to the church first and then on uphill to the site of a holy well. It continues over high pastures with dramatic views of the Scafell range of mountains. The return is made alongside the River Bleng and then back into the church to see a very rare tree.

Starting point: Gosforth free car park, well signposted in the centre of the village. Grid reference 067036.

By bus: Stagecoach Cumberland 06 from Whitehaven to Seascale. Daily except for Sundays. Infrequent service i.e. early in the morning/mid-day and late afternoon. Inquiries 0870 608 2 608.

Distance: 4½ miles

Terrain: Easy walking

Map: OS Explorer OL6, The English Lakes – South Western area.

Public toilets: In car park

Refreshments: In village

The Walk

1. **Turn left out of the car park and walk with great care along the busy road.**

☺ Pause to look across the road to a white building with small windows, the surrounds of which are painted deep red. This

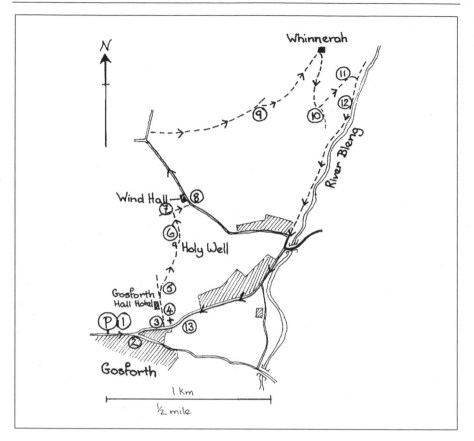

houses Gosforth library. It was built in 1628 for the Shearwen
family. In 1599, only 29 years earlier, a quarter of the 600 people
living in the parish had died of plague.

2.   **Take the first left turn and then turn left again into a hedged alley-
     way, following the signpost for the church and the Viking cross. At
     the road turn right and follow it round to come to St Mary's.**

☺ The famous sandstone cross stands in the churchyard and is just
   over 14ft (4m) high. It dates from the tenth century and has
   carvings of both Norse and Christian symbols. A story is told of a
   parishioner who was so angry that the parson was late, he
   climbed to the top of the cross and sat there. Afterwards the
   climber was confined to the stocks which stood by the cross, the
   last man to have to sit in them.

Q. Are the four sides of the cross the same? Is it square all the way down to the ground?

A. The four sides are not the same. The lower half is rounded and is said to represent an ash tree which the Norsemen believed supported the world.

☺ Can you see a man bound hand and foot who looks as if he is being punished? Look for Vidar fighting the Fenris wolf. What do you think the long animal with a twisted body and a mouth at either end represents? To help you recognise the symbols go inside the church and look at the model of the cross made by local schoolboys in 1952. Look also for the famous hogback tombs believed to be carved by the same man as did the cross. The largest stone is known as the Saint's tomb and the other as the Warrior's tomb.

Q. Why do you think the smaller is given that name?

A. Because it seems to show two armies facing each other.

Q. When and where was the bell on the window-sill captured?

A. On the Canton river in China in 1841.

3. Continue your tour of the church.

Q. Can you find the fishing stone? Why is it given that name?

A. It is next to the chancel arch and shows two people fishing for an evil serpent.

☺ Look for the 13th- and 14th-century carvings which cap the Norman pillars. The fragments of grave covers in the porch date from the same period.

Viking cross, Gosforth

4.   Leave by the side gate and turn right to walk towards Gosforth Hall Hotel. This was erected soon after the building that houses the library.

Q. What are the similarities between the two buildings?

A. Today they are painted in the same colours. They were both built of local sandstone and have the same type of small windows. Both are of the same type of structure (vernacular).

5.   Walk to the right side of the hotel to a gate with an arrow. Stride ahead to climb the next stile. Climb steadily uphill over Chapel Meadow towards the stile in the fence.

☺ To the left is all that remains of the Holy Well. Once a pilgrims' chapel stood here. Pause awhile to enjoy the glorious view of the mountains and of the bay.

6.   Beyond the stile continue uphill, keeping close beside the turf wall, on your right.

☺ The wall is constructed of cobbles and turf. Turf was used because stone was difficult to find in this area, unlike other parts of the Lake District where there are vast quantities of it and the walls are entirely of local stone.

7.   Pass through the gate in the top right corner, turn right and immediately climb a stile into a walled and fenced way to pass Wind Hall farm. From here you can glimpse the top of Wastwater Screes.

8.   At the road, turn left and walk on to a T-junction. Turn right and almost immediately turn right again to walk a long straight track. As you approach a bungalow, Bank House Park, look for two pairs of peacocks that can often be seen. You might also see fell ponies, which have very long tails, and are bred here.

9.   Go on along the track, with a spectacular view of the mountains ahead. Watch out for the sign for Whinnerah farm at the start of a wide track going off right. Follow this until just before you reach the farmhouse. Take the stile over the fence on the right and drop downhill for 50 yards (45m) to beyond a thin row of trees. Turn right to walk a wide grassy track.

☺ Look for the old gate stoop on your right, with carved slots for rails. Such stoops were used before modern-day gateposts were made. This might be the place for your picnic.

10. **Continue on downhill and then bear left beside a wall and hedge on your left to make a wide swing.**

Q. Why do you think the track has made such a zig-zagging way downhill?

A. It was once used by carts and the zig-zag reduces the gradient for the horses down such a steep slope.

11. **Continue on the indistinct way into woodland and then follow the track which becomes much clearer. Go on where it bears right and joins a narrow road. Turn right.**

12. **Stride the way, with the River Bleng (a Norse name) to your left. Look right to see why the path down the slope had to make such a huge zig-zag. When you reach a T-junction, walk ahead to join the road from Wastwater. Use the pavement side as you proceed and cross to enter the churchyard again, by a small gate.**

Q. Ahead stands a tree in a railed enclosure. What does the bark remind you of?

A. It is a cork tree, very rarely seen in the north of England. It was planted in 1833 and is still growing well.

13. **Continue through the churchyard and take the quiet road and then the track, followed on your outward route, to avoid much of the traffic on your return to the car park.**

Old gate stoop, Gosforth

2. Calder Bridge

West Cumbria has many secrets. Perhaps the greatest of all is its quietness and freedom from crowds. The village of Calder Bridge lies on the A595. It has a fine church built in 1842. Through the village runs the lovely River Calder. Two footpaths leave close to the car park; one goes through the churchyard and then takes you on a short delightful walk by the river, returning by the same route. The other crosses several pastures to Calder Abbey and also returns by the same route. Both are just over a mile in total and both are suitable for young children. For families with older children you may wish to combine the abbey walk with walks 3 and 4.

Starting point: The car park in front of the village hall, close to St Bridget's Church. Grid reference 043062.

By bus: Stagecoach Cumberland 06 service Whitehaven to Seascale. Inquiries 0870 608 2 608.

Distance: Both 1¼ miles return.

Terrain: Easy level walking.

Map: OS Explorer OL6, English Lakes – South Western area.

Public toilets: None

Refreshments: Two public houses, one with a garden overlooking the river.

NB: English Heritage has done considerable work on the abbey to make the structures safe. If you wish to visit, the custodian prefers you to phone in advance on 01946 841147 and he will take you on the tour. The entrance fee for a family might be considered too expensive and you may prefer, as suggested in the text, to look from across the pasture.

The Walk – by the river

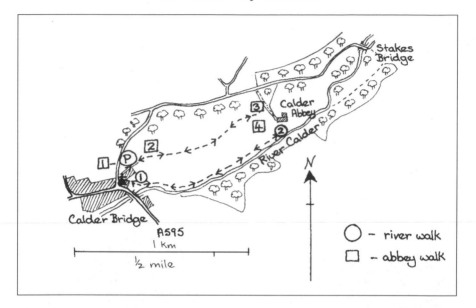

1. **Leave the village centre by the signpost directing you through the church-yard. Stroll on beside the river passing below a variety of lofty trees.**

Q. What are the four-lobed open cases, or husks, found strewn over the footpath below several of the tall beech trees?

A. They are the fruit of the beech trees. Each husk has a coating of hairs. When the husk is ripe it opens to release two shiny tri-angular nuts, which are the tree's seeds.

Beech Nuts

2.   **Continue until you reach a fence with a 'Private' notice on it. Return the same way.**

😊 Notice the varying depths of the river. Where it comes close to the nearer bank it is shallow and there are small exposed beds of red gravel. On the far side, where the rock face descends sheer into the water the river is very deep. Look at the colour of the rock face. It is sandstone, as is the gravel, and similar in colour to the stone used to build the church and some of the houses in the village.

The Walk – to the abbey

Calder Abbey

1.   **Take the reinforced way at the side of the petrol station, beside the car park. It is signposted 'Stakes Bridge via Monks Road'. Continue between several houses and then bear right. Almost immediately take the narrow track on your left.**

Q.   What is the plant growing on the old gate at the start of the little track?

A.   Ivy

2. Climb the stile and walk ahead, with the wall and fence to your left, to climb the next one. Continue on towards the buildings ahead. Pass through a gate and walk ahead, keeping to the left of the rather forbidding gatehouse of the abbey. Stroll on to a stile. Cross the grass to join a track.

☺ Notice the fine avenue of trees lining the track. Look for the tall beeches with their smooth pale grey bark, which never becomes rough whatever the age of the tree. There are also some fine horse-chestnut trees. These are easy to recognise by their buds, leaves and fruit. Another way to identify them is by their graceful branches, which curve downwards, turning up at the ends.

3. From the track look across the pasture to the ruins of Calder Abbey.

Q. How many arches of the nave can you see?
A. Five.

☺ The fine tower is 64ft (20m) tall but once was half as high again. Lofty walls and fine arches are all that remains of the abbey, a daughter monastic house of Furness Abbey. It was founded in 1134 as a Benedictine monastery, which 14 years later joined the Cistercians. It survived until 1536, when it was dissolved on the orders of Henry VIII. Across the pasture you can see the bakehouse of the abbey and another small building that once housed the electricity generator used by Calder House mansion, which was built on part of the ancient walls of the abbey.

4. Return by your outward route.

3. Thornholme

This is a most satisfactory walk that takes you from deciduous woodland in the valley of the River Calder to high on slopes above the wide dancing river. Near Thornholme, a charming isolated farmhouse, you cross the river and a beck and then return on an airy fell road, gated and unfenced for much of the way. The National Park has put in good stiles and a footbridge, and the route is well waymarked. This four-mile walk could be joined with the previous walk or added to the walk which follows.

Starting point: A large lay-by just beyond Stakes Bridge over the River Calder. Grid reference 056067. To reach this parking area, leave the A595 by a right turn at Calder Bridge. In just over half-a-mile, and where the road turns sharp left, continue ahead along a narrow 'no through road'.

By bus: See walk 1 for details of buses to Calder Bridge. Inquiries 0870 608 2 608.

Distance: 4 miles

Terrain: Easy walking all the way. After rain the track below Strudda Bank farm can be muddy.

Map: OS Explorer OL6, The English Lakes – South Western area.

Public toilets: None on walk

Refreshments: None on walk

The Walk

1. **From the parking area, recross Stakes Bridge.**

Q. Under how many arches does the river flow?

A. Two

2. **Walk on to take a signposted stile on the right into Calder Woodlands. Stroll the delightful track through oak, beech and hazel. Where the track divides, keep to the right branch that takes you well**

above the river. As you continue watch out for the small signpost, directing you left, uphill on a narrow path, through the trees.

Q. On the bark of the trees is a coating of green vegetation, which is composed of algae, lichen and moss. Does this green mat go right round the trunks?

A. No

Q. Can you suggest a reason why it is found where it is?

A. It grows on the side of the trunk facing west, from which direction it receives most rain. Water is essential for the tiny, lowly plants to thrive.

3. Follow this gently rising path to a stile on the edge of the trees. Beyond, bear right and follow the wall on your right. As you near the

corner and the wall bears left, cut across the corner (to avoid a muddy hollow) and carry on with the continuing wall to your right. At the next corner, climb two stiles and drop down the slope carefully. Cross a small beck and climb up to a stile.

4. Press on the stiled way and enjoy the extensive view of the fells ahead. Watch out for the stile on your right which gives access to a fenced track. Carry on with a fence to the right. Ignore the footpath that drops steeply downhill to the river. Continue ahead with the hedge to your left.

5. Just beyond the farm gate on the left watch for the track leaving the hedge and beginning its gentle descent, through scattered gorse. Pass through the gate and go on down to a sheepfold. Here follow the path as it swings left and climbs up the slope to a stile in the fence. Once over walk ahead. Beyond the fence on the right the land drops steeply down to the hurrying river.

6. Beyond the next stile the path drops down to a footbridge over the river.

☺ The River Calder rises on Lank Rigg, one of the bleak heights to the south of Ennerdale Water and flows into the sea near Calder Hall.

7. Go over the bridge, walk ahead and pass through the gate on your left. Cross the next bridge across Worm Gill.

Q. What do you call the junction of two rivers?

Stakes Bridge

A. A confluence.

Q. Before the bridges were constructed how do you think travellers crossed the rivers?

A. On foot over the ford – difficult and dangerous if the river was in spate.

8. Look for the indistinct track climbing uphill. It is easier to find the way if you look for the exit from the ford. Climb gently passing to the right of Thornholme farmhouse. At the fell road, turn right and walk the hill.

☺ From the brow you can see the towers of the world's first full-scale nuclear power station. The Windscale plant opened in 1951, for the production of plutonium, followed in 1956 by Calder Hall power station for producing electricity.

9. Stride the gated fell road as it steadily descends. Look across the deep valley of the Calder to see where you walked earlier.

☺ Notice the wall along the roadside. It is composed of two rows of Eskdale granite, a pinkish rock which is rough to touch and which weathers to rounded cobbles. Look for the squarer boulders which tie the two sides together.

10. Go on to pass High Prior Scales farm.

☺ Here look for a modern barn for storing hay, which you pass first, and then the much older barn built of warm red stone, with exceptionally thick walls. Can you spot a face on the building?

Q. What do you think is the purpose of the rows of square holes up close to the roof?

A. For pigeons to enter a loft.

11. Stride on the quiet road until you rejoin your car.

Pigeon holes in barn, Prior Scales

4. Monks Bridge, Kinniside Common

This short walk along a rough track takes you into a quiet hollow in the moorland of Kinniside Common to visit the glorious Monks Bridge. It arches, like a bridge for fairies, across a narrow deep chasm and is just wide enough for a packhorse to cross. The monks of Calder Abbey would have crossed it on their many journeys. Iron ore would have been carried over the bridge, perhaps from Ennerdale, to bloomeries, or smithies, on the fells to be smelted. The monks most likely built the bridge (an easy job after the abbey) for use when the River Calder was in spate and the ford, 200m downstream, was impassable. The bridge is also known as Matty Benn's bridge and sometimes Hannah Benn's. The Benn families lived nearby. Its other name is High Wath, meaning a high ford. You might wish to add the visit to Monks Bridge on to the last walk. If so continue from the first bridge crossed below Thornholme farm, and go on ahead on a path that winds right, round the side of the large knoll that lies to the right of the River Calder. The way soon becomes a wide track, which climbs uphill and then descends to the ford and the footbridge over the river. Do not cross but head upstream for 200m to see the packhorse bridge. To continue the combined walk return by the same track and path and cross the second bridge below Thornholme farm.

Starting point: Close to the National Trust board on Kinniside Common. Grid reference 055101. This lies on moorland on the east side of Cold Fell Road, approximately half-way between the villages of Calder Bridge and Ennerdale.

By bus: No public transport

Distance: 2 miles

Terrain: Rough track to the side of the Calder. A little scrambling is required to reach the bridge where, after rain, you can expect plenty of mud.

Map: OS Explorer OL6, English Lakes – South Western area.

Public toilets: Villages of Ennerdale or Calder Bridge.

Refreshments: In the above villages.

Monks Bridge

The Walk

1. From the parking area walk down the track, with Friar Gill to your right. Where the path divides take the right fork.

Q. Why do you think there is a barrier over the track?

A. To prevent vehicles using a track which is not suitable for such traffic.

2. Cross a small stream and go on to pause by a small quarry. Notice the thin layer of soil and vegetation overlying the solid rock below.

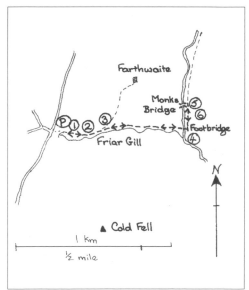

Q. Why do you think the ground on both sides of the track is so wet for much of the winter and after rain in the summer?

A. Because the water is prevented from draining away by the rock below the thin soil cover. This is true for most of the pasture you can see.

3. Pass through the gate and notice the sheep pens on either side of the beck. Cross the River Calder by the sturdy footbridge. Look downstream to see the ford.

4. Turn left and head upstream, moving away from the beck to cross a narrow shallow ford over Caplecrag Beck.

5. WITH CHILDREN UNDER TIGHT CONTROL descend to the side of the bridge. There is no right of way across it.

Q. Why do you think it has no parapets?

A. They would get in the way of the panniers carried by the packhorses.

Q. Look with great care to the opposite bank to see ladder fern growing. Why do you think it is given this name?

A. Because the fronds look like tiny ladders.

6. Return to your car by the same route if you have not combined the two walks.

Ladder Fern

5. St Bees Head

Cumbria has a coastline as well as mountains, lakes, rivers, woodlands and delectable dales. Just north of the charming village of St Bees, it erupts in spectacular cliffs, all part of the St Bees Head nature reserve. This delightful 5 mile walk takes you along the flower-bedecked cliff path, visits the lonely Fleswick Bay, looks in on precariously nesting seabirds, passes a lighthouse and visits an ancient church. Much of the path is fenced on the sea side but parts are not and children need to be reminded to walk with care. Choose a good day – little wind and lots of sun – when the combination of the deep blue sea and the lovely red sandstone cliffs is incomparable.

Starting point: Pay-and-display (except Sundays and bank holidays) car park above the sandy beach at St Bees village. Grid reference 961118. The well signposted village lies five miles south of Whitehaven.

By bus: Very limited. Stagecoach Cumberland bus 20 Whitehaven to St Bees. Inquiries 0870 608 2 608.

Distance: 5 miles

Terrain: Steep climb at start of walk and another onto St Bees Head but paths though narrow are easy to walk and to follow.

Map: OS Explorer 303.

Public toilets: On car park

Refreshments: Four public houses in the village. The French Connection restaurant situated in the old Victorian station. The Seacote Hotel near the beach.

The Walk

On the green, beyond the car park, is a children's playground. Standing on the green is an information board. It tells you several interesting facts about the area.

Q. What famous long distance walk starts from the sea wall?
A. Alfred Wainwright's Coast to Coast.

Q. Where does it end?
A. Robin Hood's Bay on the North Yorkshire coast.

Q. How long is the walk?
A. 190 miles.

Q: What does Wainwright urge walkers to do before setting off on this long walk?
A. To wet their boots in the Irish Sea.

1. **Walk north (towards the cliffs) along the short promenade. Cross the Rottington Beck by a wide footbridge and bear right. Ignore the ladder-stile on the right and follow the signpost directions for St Bees Head. Begin to climb the steep stepped slope that ascends the sandstone cliffs.**

😊 In summer large clumps of scabious, sea thrift and silver weed line the way. Meadow pipits call sweetly from the fencing posts and a merlin might be seen flying fast between the flowering gorse. A merlin is the smallest of the falcons. It is especially fond of catching beetles and moths for its food. The male is a slate-blue colour and the female brown.

2. **Continue on the long path, with great care if small children are in the party, until you reach a stile in the fence on your right. Take this and walk on, inside the fence, to the next stile, which you do not cross. If you miss the first stile take extreme care as you approach the second stile, outside the fence, as the path ends at the cliff edge.**

3. **Look for your first glimpse of Fleswick Bay. Beyond the next ladder-stile, begin your gentle descent, inside the fence. Look for more glorious flowers growing on the cliff edge, behind the fence.**

Q. Why do you think the flowers thrive beyond the fence and very few on the pasture?
A. The fence protects them from the hungry sheep.

4. **Follow the waymarked steps down the slope to a shallow ravine. Turn left to scramble over the great slabs of sandstone to the beach. Take care where the stone is wet and slippery.**

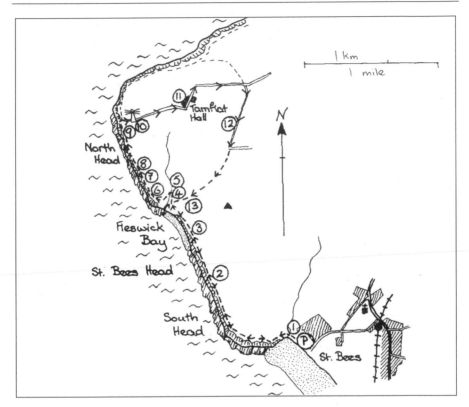

☺ Here on the beach you should see rock pipits hunting flies among the masses of wall pennywort growing on the rocks. Look south to see (if it is the right time of year) innumerable herring gulls, intent on their chicks, perched on every small ledge. The air rings with their raucous calls. Spend some time searching among the shingle for the semi-precious stones reputed to be present. To the north of the bay, rearing upwards, stands St Bees Head, a huge sandstone cliff. Caves at its foot were used by smugglers.

5.   Return along the ravine and cross the waymarked stile over the fence on the left. Climb the stepped way and head towards the fence at the edge of the cliff. Beyond, in summertime, is another glorious flower garden where you should see brightly coloured bloody cranesbill, soft-pink rest harrow and yellow common melilot. From here you also have another good view of the bay and its huge slabs of sandstone.

6. Keep up beside the fence to the top of the slope and above the gorse bushes. Look right to see a large white seat just made for your picnic.

7. Return to the fence and continue on the almost level way to a stile in the fence which gives access to an observation platform. Again young children and dogs should be under control.

☺ From the platform you have a magnificent view of a huge cliff face, where from April onwards you should see many birds beginning to establish their territories, each claiming a small portion of ledge. Look out for fulmars, which sail in on wings stiff like those of a glider. You should see and hear kittiwakes, small white gulls with black-tipped grey wings. They call their names constantly. Further down the cliff face you might spot a line of guillemots, all facing into the cliff face. You might even see the black guillemots, which do breed here; they have a big white patch on the wing and brilliant red legs.

8. Stroll on to the next observation platform and watch for razor-bills. Continue on beside the fence to the next viewing platform.

☺ Look carefully from here, at the right time of the year, to see black and white puffins far below on a wide ledge shaded darkly by an overhang. The birds stand upright on their bright vermillion legs, round-eyed and serious-looking. If one turns a little you might get a glimpse of its multi-coloured bill.

9. Walk on. If it is clear out to sea you should see the Isle of Man, and the hills of Galloway to the north. At the fourth platform great care should be taken because part of the cliff is unfenced and there is a no-

St Bees Head

tice saying so. Continue to a small white painted building ahead. This houses the foghorn of the lighthouse.

10. Here turn right and walk inland towards the lighthouse. Beyond a gate the track becomes a lane and leads out into the countryside, where sheep and cattle graze. Here you are likely to see swallows and house martins.

Q. Why do you think they are swooping low over the pastures?

A. They are after flies and insects which tend to hover just above the ground, attracted by the presence of farm animals.

Q. Can you see any swallows on the ground – look for them perching on the edge of a muddy puddle? What are they doing?

A. They are collecting mud for their nests. They have very short legs and do not perch easily.

11. Pass between farm buildings and go in front of two houses and walk on. Where the road swings sharply to the left look for a covered reservoir on the right. Leave the lane and take a signposted cart track on the right that runs beside the reservoir.

12. Climb a high ladder-stile and continue to the next one, which you also climb. Walk on to a gate ahead. Beyond continue beside the wall on your left, dropping steadily downhill until you attain the stile to the head of the little ravine leading to Fleswick Bay.

13. From here return left along the cliff path to St Bees.

☺ As you drive away from the beach you might still have time to visit the Priory Church, with its fine Norman arch over the west door. Set among flowering grasses in the overgrown graveyard is a small stone pillar with ornate patterning – the base of a Viking cross.

Guillemot and Razor-bill

6. Smithy Beck Forest Trail, Ennerdale

Smithy Beck Forest Trail combines a pleasing walk beside Ennerdale Water with a waymarked trail through the forest. Clearings, carpeted with heather thriving between outcrops of rock, reveal wonderful views of the surrounding fells. This is an exciting trek for children, with its narrow up-and-down paths, its 'secret' clearing – once the site of a medieval settlement – and its two magnificent viewpoints overlooking the lake. The trail divides into two parts. The shorter takes about an hour at a steady pace and the full trail, twice as long, explores higher parts. The trail is waymarked in red and the markers add to the fun, with youngsters finding the route. A pamphlet can be obtained from the Forestry Commission or from the National Trust warden, who is often to be found in the car park. There are eight numbered stops along the way and the pamphlet explains the points interest at each stop. Similar points of interest are included in the text of this walk if you are unable to obtain a leaflet.

Starting point: Bowness Knott car park. Grid reference 109154. This lies on the north side of Ennerdale Water at the end of the road; vehicles are not allowed beyond the car park. At the village of Ennerdale Bridge take the narrow road leading to the lake. Where the road divides take the left fork and continue on through pastures. The parking area lies 3¼ miles from the village.

By bus: No public transport.

Distance: Shorter walk 2 miles. Longer walk 3½ miles.

Terrain: Generally easy walking.

Map: OS Explorer OL4, The English Lakes – North Western area.

Public toilets: In car park.

Refreshments: In Ennerdale village.

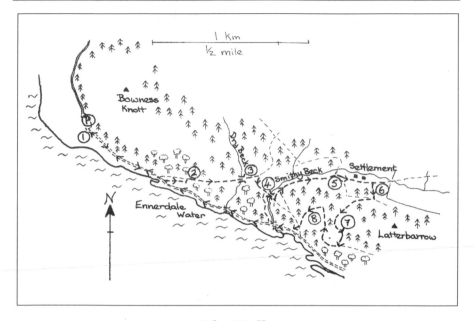

The Walk

1. **Leave the car park and walk the forest road towards the head of the lake. At the first small picnic site, take the trail, climbing left through trees. Turn right along a forest ride bordered with larch on the right and Scots pine growing on the steeper slopes to your left. (Stop 1.)**

☺ Holly, juniper, oak, rowan, birch and hawthorn grow between the taller trees. On the floor of the forest look for lichens, liverworts and mosses.

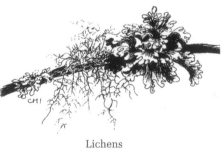

Lichens

Q. Can you think of a reason why these lowly plants thrive so well?

A. Because the young trees form a blanket over them, trapping warmth, raising the moisture in the air and protecting them from the wind.

2. **Follow the gently climbing ride to come to the side of Dry Beck. (Stop 2.)**

😊 It is called Dry Beck because what water it does have percolates through the boulders of the bed and is lost to sight. Where the water empties into the lake you can hear it hurrying below the rocks, but again there is nothing to be seen.

3.   Cross the footbridge and stride on, still ascending. Look out for where the trail leaves the forest road, makes a sharp right turn and descends to the side of Smithy Beck. (Stop 3.) The trail divides at this point and you may decide to return at this point. In that case ignore the footbridge over the beck and descend to the lake side, where you turn right to return to the car park.

4.   To continue on the longer walk, cross the footbridge and pause to enjoy the splendid waterfall to your left. Then climb the opposite bank of Smithy Beck to turn left along a track to the forest road, where you turn left again.

😊 As you go notice the variation in height of the trees all planted in the same year.

Q.   Can you think of a reason for this variation?

A.   The roots of the trees have had to compete with the roots of other plants. The drainage is poor here and the lack of air around the roots has resulted in little or no growth.

😊 Then you come to an area of peat moorland. (Stop 4). You have climbed steadily until you are now above the 600ft (183m) contour line on the OS map, where in the north and west of the British Isles you can expect high rainfall and not much sunshine to dry it up. The rain takes the goodness out of the soil and carries both down the steep slopes, causing erosion and leaving the soil acid. This is

Head of Ennerdale

poor soil for farming but it can grow some very good trees if it is ploughed and given back some nutrients.

5.   **Where the forest road divides and turns left or right, look for a narrow path, with a notice board, continuing ahead into a clearing.**

☺ Here were medieval dwellings or shielings, occupied by farmers who also mined iron ore. The original forest was oak, alder, birch and hazel. It was felled by the farmers to produce the charcoal they needed to smelt the ores. They produced the charcoal by slow 'burning' in pitsteads scattered through the forest. The charcoal was then carried by ponies to the mouth of Smithy Beck, where the iron was smelted in a bloomery.

6.   **Go on almost to the end of the clearing and then turn right to climb a wide grassy ride through a plantation, originally of Lodgepole pine. (Stop 6.)**

☺ During a storm in 1984 gale force winds blew many down. The area has been planted with larch and deciduous trees. As you climb notice the tiny feathery plants growing on the larch.

Q.   Can you name these plants?

A.   They are lichens and they thrive in the pure, damp air.

7.   **The lovely way continues to a splendid viewpoint. (Stop 7 and a notice board telling you the Ennerdale Story.) If the sun is shining this is the place for your picnic.**

☺ Look down with care to see oak trees thriving. These have grown naturally from seed into seedlings and then into young saplings.

Q.   As they developed they were fenced around. Can you suggest why?

A.   To protect them from hungry sheep.

8.   **Descend the well graded path, over the shoulder of Latterbarrow, towards the lake. Pause to enjoy the spectacular views. Cross a forest road (Stop 8) and then follow a path to join the main forest road. Turn right to return to the car park.**

☺ As you go look for pieces of slag on the shore at the mouth of Smithy Beck, all that remains of the bloomery. Listen for the hidden water of Dry Beck.

7. Liza Beck, Ennerdale

Ennerdale Water, one of the most remote and inaccessible of the lakes, provides a pleasing walk for those wanting to escape noise and bustle. No road runs beside its tranquil water, no private craft disturbs its placid surface. Once its serried ranks of conifers made much of the dale a forbidding place, but now its lines have been softened by the landscaping and mixed planting policy adopted by the Forestry Commission.

This walk, after starting from the car park and crossing Char Dub, follows the green waymarked trail, which was constructed in 1985, beside the River Liza on its southern side. It continues to the concrete forest road bridge, returning along the forest road on the northern side of the river.

Starting point: Bowness Knott car park. Grid reference 109154. (See walk 5).

By bus: No public transport.

Distance: 7 miles

Terrain: Easy walking.

Map: OS Explorer OL4, The English Lakes – North Western area.

Public toilets: In car park.

Refreshments: Ennerdale village.

Little Bridge, Ennerdale

The Walk

1. Leave the car park and continue along the forest road for just over 1½ miles. Look for the concrete bridge spanning Char Dub.

2. Do not cross the bridge but go on to follow the blue and green waymarked post directing you down the slope on your right to cross a footbridge over the River Liza. Continue on the waymarked path almost to the forest track on the southern side of the river.

3. Do not miss the glorious green waymarked path that goes off left, to join a forest track over Little Irish Bridge. Look for the sign on the left directing you left on a forest track past great banks of heather, between the river and the forest.

☺ Most of the trail lies over the Ennerdale Granophyre, a warm pink-coloured hard volcanic rock which breaks into blocks.

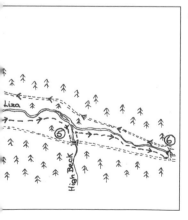

4. Continue on. Look out for Moss Dub, a tarn on your right, edged with birch and rhododendrons. Towards the end of the pretty sheet of water, descend steps on your left. Stride on to the side of Low Beck and walk right. Do not be confused by the small footbridge ahead, which is on the opposite bank of the river and cannot be reached. Go on to the forest road, cross a bridge and turn immediately left to walk the opposite bank of Low Beck. Cross the footbridge seen earlier.

☺ Here you might see roe deer. These small mammals browse the tops of pine shoots, leaving frayed edges. They also graze yew and gorse. Their droppings, black to dark brown and deposited in heaps, are easily confused with those of sheep.

Roe deer

5. Stroll on, with a dramatic view of Pillar mountain ahead, to reach the side of High Beck. Walk right, beside it, before crossing a footbridge. Beyond bear left and proceed beside the Liza with its many rocky pools and small waterfalls. At the forest road you join the blue Nine Becks trail. Bear left to cross a concrete bridge.

Q. What does the information board tell you about future plans for the forest?

A. As areas are cleared of conifers Forest Enterprise hopes to plant a much greater variety of trees and to leave far more open spaces.

6. Turn left and begin your return along the wide forest road, enjoying the magnificent views as you go. Continue past the bridge and follow the road along the lake shore As you near the car park, the road climbs away right from the lake.

☺ Tree planting in Ennerdale started in 1926 to help create a reserve of timber and to provide work for the unemployed miners of Cleator Moor. Today the forest is a haven for wildlife.

8. Warnscale Beck and Dubs Quarry at the head of Buttermere

This is an energetic walk into the heart of the mountains, where the Warnscale Beck hurries between steep gorges. The slopes of Fleetwith Pike, to your left, are largely scree-covered but support a few weather-worn hawthorns, holly, yew and bleached rowans. Mist often tangles with the tops of Haystacks, the mountain to the right of the beck, which shows a great wall of crags to the walker. Lowly plants cover the higher slopes of this exciting hidden corner of Lakeland, bracken thrives in Warnscale Bottom and rowans and heather cling precariously to the sides of miniature canyons which cradle the beck.

As you climb you feel you might be the first human to have ventured this way. And yet the tracks on both sides of the beck were made by quarrymen for their ponies to bring down slate and would once have resounded to their noise and have been very busy. Close to the source of the beck there is a huge mass of evidence of their activities.

As you climb spare a thought for the quarrymen and their ponies, as they did the same walk, perhaps several times a day, most days of the week and in all kinds of weather.

Before you return from the site of Dubs Quarry you may wish to extend your walk by following a clearly cairned track right to visit Blackbeck Tarn and then on to Innominate Tarn, both pleasing pools to be found in heather clad hollows and set amid lichen-clad outcrops.

Families with well motivated youngsters might be tempted to go on to the summit of Haystacks, 1900ft (582m), and then return to Dubs Quarry. But families with young children should not attempt it. Older youngsters will enjoy descending by way of the summit, using the pitched path that descends steeply to Scarth Gap, a sort of half-way point, and then continuing, right, down more pitched track to the valley bottom.

Starting point: Gatesgarthdale car park at the foot of Honister Pass. Grid reference 195149. Use the honesty box for payment.

By bus: Stagecoach Cumberland, 77A, Keswick via Honister (summer service only). Alight at the car park. Inquiries 0870 608 2 608

Distance: To Dubs quarry and back 3½ miles. To
                       Innominate Tarn add another 1½ miles. To the summit of
                       Haystacks and returning via Dubs Quarry add another
                       half mile. If you descend from Haystacks via Scarth Gap,
                       the circular walk is 5 miles long.

Terrain: The first three-quarters of a mile is a delightful level walk.
                       Then follows a steady climb along a cairned way. Around
                       Blackbeck and Innominate Tarns are pleasing rocky
                       outcrops and small grassy areas, where children will
                       enjoy scrambling, and there are good places for a picnic.
                       The return down the quarry track is enjoyable but at one
                       place young children should be under close control. This
                       is not a walk for poor weather. Choose a long sunny day
                       when the heather is in bloom.

Map: OS Explorer OL4, The English Lakes – North Western
                       area.

Refreshments and toilets: Buttermere village. Keswick. There is often an
                       ice-cream van near the car park.

The Walk

1. **From the car park, turn left to climb the road leading to the pass.**

Q. What are the trees growing on the left of the road and those
     growing on the right?

A. Scots pine and sycamore.

☺ Sycamores are native throughout Central Europe and were not
   introduced into England until the 15th century. They are tall trees
   with stout trunks. They grow happily on most soils and can
   withstand buffeting winds during storms. They are used as shelter
   belt trees around exposed hill farms.

2. **Take the signposted bridleway on the right just past Gatesgarth Cot-
    tages on the right. As you stroll the pleasing track, look ahead to the
    striking serrated-topped Haystacks mountain. Look for the white
    cross on the slopes of Fleetwith Pike to your left, which was erected to
    commemorate Fanny Mercer (see walk 9). After three-quarters of a
    mile leave the track to take a grassy trod through bracken to cross a
    wooden footbridge over Warnscale Beck. The path continues beside
    the stream and then, just before a pleasing waterfall, takes a sharp
    right turn.**

Haystacks from Warnscale Dub

3. **Follow the old quarry path as it climbs in a series of zig-zags below the forbidding face of Haystacks. Look for a breach in the skyline through which descends Black Beck. It has issued out of the first tarn you might wish to visit. The path continues past the old buildings of the disused Green Crag quarry – Green Crag towers above you.**

☺ From the quarry slate was obtained. Slate is a hard rock which can be split into smooth thin layers. It is composed of clay and shale that have been compressed by great pressure or great heat.

4. **Continue climbing. The cairned way leads you to a junction of paths. If you wish to visit Blackbeck Tarn and then on to Innominate, turn right and follow the rough cairned path. To continue on the shorter walk, turn left to descend below a rocky crag on a good reinforced path to stepping stones that take you across Warnscale Beck. Pause here to see the great spoil heaps of Dubs Quarry.**

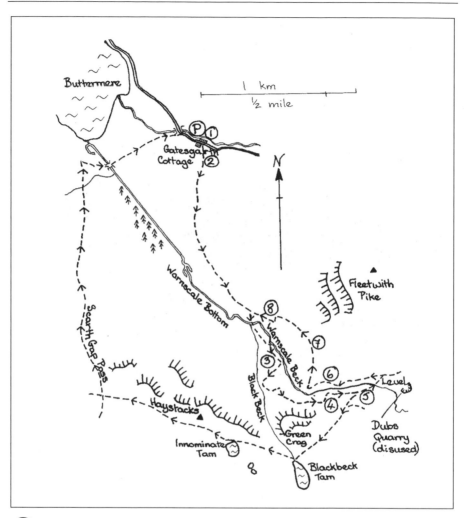

☺ Close by the spoil heaps is the marshy area of Dubs Bottom. Here quarry workers lived in small rough huts during the week, returning to their families at the weekends. They kept carrier pigeons.

Q. Can you suggest why?

A. To send messages to their families.

5. **Follow the reinforced path up the slope towards a ruined quarry building to join a wide track, where you turn left. It is well cairned,**

extremely well reinforced and always finds the easiest way down. It passes through great banks of sweet smelling heather.

☺ Look left to see two quarry holes (part of Green Crag Quarry, passed earlier). Much of the slate had to be 'mined' as it was deeply bedded and these were known as 'closehead' workings, where the slaters worked by candlelight and in difficult conditions. Slate can be bluish, grey or green rock and is used for roofing or for floors. Dubs Quarry produced green slate.

6. **As you edge round a crag, youngsters need to be under control because though the track is wide there is a drop to the left. Then the track continues steadily downhill.**

☺ As you go look for traces of old pitching (see Walk 26).

Q. Why do you think the track descends so gradually and has obviously had much work done on its surface in years gone by.

A. It needed to have a gradual slope and a good surface as it would have been used by ponies to bring down slate.

7. **As you descend look for the meandering Warnscale Beck sparkling in the sunlight.**

Q. Why do you think the course of the beck has been straightened so that it flows in a straight line into Buttermere? The pastures to its right will give you a clue.

A. It has been straightened to provide drainage so that the pastures could be reclaimed from marsh. This has provided more good ground for the farmer at Gatesgarth farm.

8. **Join the track used on your outward journey to walk through Warnscale Bottom. These pastures were created thousands of years ago from silt washed down from the mountain slopes.**

9. Buttermere

Buttermere: the name conjures up a picture of tranquil water, crags rising sharply, mixed woodland, delightful lakeside paths, foaming becks racing down steep slopes, tree creepers, tufted ducks and a clear translucent light. Sometimes the water of the lake is quite green as a result of slate dust washed down from the quarries above.

This superb five-mile walk, which takes you around the lake, will be enjoyed by all the family. The paths are well maintained and as you stroll the ever-changing views are spectacular.

Starting point:	There are two pay-and-display car parks in Buttermere. The National Park's lies behind the Fish Hotel in the centre of the village and the National Trust's on the B5289 as it enters the village from the north-west end. This walk starts from the latter.
By bus:	Stagecoach Cumberland, 77A, Keswick via Honister Pass. Inquiries 0870 608 2 608.
Distance:	5 miles
Terrain:	Level footpaths and tracks for most of the way. On one small stretch along the B-road, children should take care as the road can be busy in the summer.
Map:	OS Explorer OL4, The English Lakes – North Western area.

Refreshments and toilets: Buttermere village.

The Walk

1. From the car park, turn right and descend, with care, the short slope into the village. Ignore the right turn and climb up the slope with the village hall to your left.

☺ This colourful single-storey building was once the village school but it is 46 years since the bell last rang to summon its pupils to lessons. Sometimes the age range of children stretched from four to 14 and the numbers fluctuated between 2 and 16. When the school opened in the late 19th century, a coke-burning stove

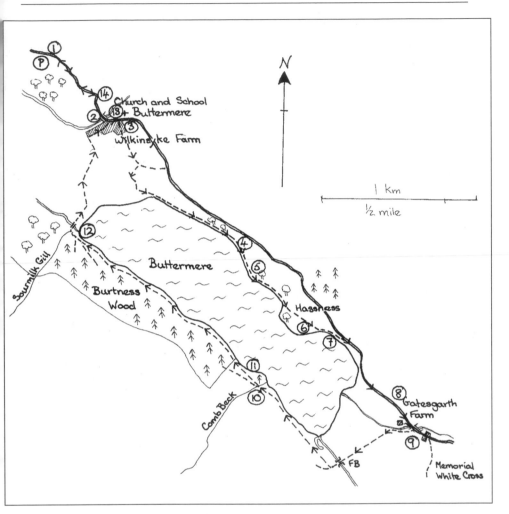

provided warmth in winter. For hand washing three enamel bowls were supplied – one for the girls, one for the boys and the other for the teacher. The toilet was a bucket under a wooden seat.

2. **Where the road swings sharp left, look for the public bridleway sign for the lake shore, going off right. It passes in front of a farmhouse, with farm buildings to the right. Continue on past the next dwelling to climb the stile to the right of a gate. Stroll the continuing path, with Robinson the tall mountain to your left. Pause here to look right, across the lake, to see a seemingly thin silvery ribbon of water dropping perpendicularly through larch.**

Q. Why do you think the waterfall is called Sourmilk?

A. Because when it is in spate, the beck foams creamy white and looks like sour milk.

3. **Follow the small signpost directing you right along a fenced path, which leads you round rocks to a path close to the lovely lake. Stride the permitted footpath to pass through some tall trees.**

Q. Can you name these?

A. Oaks (see Walk 19).

4. **Go on to the next stile, where there is a notice board**

Q. For how many years is free-access allowed across the pasture just above the shore?

A. Ten years.

5. **Ahead lies a tunnel through an imposing crag. Go through it.**

☺ The passage was hewn in the 19th century for George Benson, a Manchester mill-owner, the then owner of the large white house in the trees to your left. He wanted to be able to walk along the shore without having to climb the crag at the water's edge. He also did not want his workmen remaining idle on wet days and so set them to hew the tunnel. It is nearly six feet (1.8m) high and 30 feet (9m) long and is rather damp. It has a wonderful echo.

6. **Go on to pass through the kissing gate, which has remnants of some pleasing wrought-iron work.**

☺ On the other side of the lake you can see another waterfall, this one on Comb Beck. The lively stream rises in Burtness Comb below the serrated edges of Comb Crags. A comb is a bowl-shaped hollow scooped and rounded by a glacier during the last ice-age. Perhaps you can spot the comb high above the lace-like curtain of white foam.

7. **Continue past a beach of shingle and then on to the road along which you continue. Make full use of the grassy verge as you go and go with care.**

☺ At a safe point, look ahead to see Fleetwith Pike, the shapely conical hill ahead. Look for the white cross on the lower slope – it lies just above the tops of the trees in the foreground. This is a memorial to a woman named Fanny Mercer, who when climbing the slopes in 1887, tripped over her Victorian equivalent of today's telescopic walking pole and fell to her death.

8. Cross the road bridge over Gatesgarthdale Beck, and turn right into a signposted footpath to walk beside the beck.

Q. What is the meaning of the blue and white disc, with a white cross on a red background, fixed to the gate post?

A. It stands for a mountain rescue post.

9. Take the path signposted 'lakeside' and continue ahead. Cross the beck by a footbridge. Go on through a gate and turn right to begin your return along the opposite side of the lake. The path keeps well above the sparkling water and gives you a good view of where you have walked earlier. You also have a dramatic view of the austere mountains that edge this pretty lake.

10. Cross the footbridge over Comb Beck which you looked at earlier from the opposite shore. At the signpost take the permitted path that directs you towards the edge of the lake. Pass through the gate into Burtness Wood.

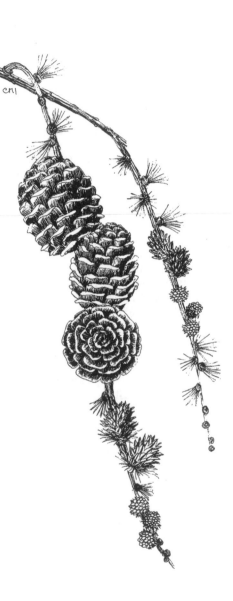

Larch

Q. What are the trees that form the plantation?

A. Larch.

☺ Larch unfolds its green tassels of needles in March. Scattered among these are pink 'roses'. These are the female flowers of the tree and eventually form the familiar cones. Larch timber is very strong and is good for use out-of-doors as fencing, gates and bridges and for boat building.

11. Where the path branches, take the right fork, leading towards the water's edge. You might wish to sit on the seat to enjoy another glorious view. Go on along the pleasing track. Just before the wall ahead, take the gate on the right, cross the footbridge and pause to look up Sourmilk Gill, also seen earlier.

12. Cross the next footbridge over Buttermere Dubs and continue to walk the fenced path into the village. Pass the Fish Hotel.

☺ It was here that Mary Harrison, known as the Beauty of Buttermere, lived. She attracted the attention of a man named John Hadfield, who was a fraudster, and already married. In all innocence she married him. Eventually his past caught up with him and he was sent to trial at Carlisle, not for bigamy but for defrauding the post office. This was considered a very serious crime and he was hanged. Mary eventually married a man from Caldbeck and you pass her home on walk 25. She is buried in Caldbeck Church, also visited on the same walk.

13. Walk on to the T-junction. Bear right and continue uphill to the little church of St James, which lies behind and above the old school passed at the outset of the walk.

☺ The parishioners in the 18th century were so poor they could not support a priest and the village was served by unordained men called readers. One of these was 'Wonderful Walker', Robert Walker of Seathwaite. He served Buttermere until 1736. His stipend, or wage, was £1 a year so it had to be supplemented by work as a teacher, labourer, spinner and scrivener (someone who wrote letters and documents for those who could not write). He took advantage of the custom of 'whittlegate', which entitled him to share the home of each family in the parish for a fortnight or so.

Q. Look for the plaque in the window on the right. Who does it commemorate? What was he famous for? What is the name of the mountain you can see out of the window? Why was the plaque placed there?

A. Albert Wainwright. Walking guides. Haystacks. Wainwright's favourite fell.

☺ Haystacks is the mountain you walked very close to or visited on walk 8.

14. **Return from the church, pass the old school on your right and continue up the hill to return to the car park.**

Iron post, Buttermere

10. Crummock Water

This is the longest walk in the book and also one of the most beautiful. At 8½ miles (12km), and taking 5 to 6 hours, it could be too long for young children. Perhaps two small families could make use of two cars, leaving one at Scale Hill car park and the other at Buttermere, completing the all-round walk over two days.

Crummock Water shares the same valley with Buttermere and tall mountains rise up steeply from the shores of both lakes. The village of Buttermere sits between the two on the only flat area large enough for farmhouses, hotels, a church and an old school, the latter now the village hall.

At the foot of the lake, where the River Cocker hastens on its way towards Cockermouth, there are sluice gates, footbridges, fish ladders and a hexagonal pumping house, which help in controlling the level of the lake that supplies Workington's water needs. When the lake is high after much rain, the outflow from lake to river is dramatic and impressive.

Starting point:	The easy-to-miss National Trust pay-and-display car park at Scalehill Bridge at the north end of Crummock Water. It lies on the east side of the River Cocker. Grid reference 149215.
By bus:	Cumberland Stagecoach 77, Keswick, Lorton, Buttermere. Summer service only. This bus allows you just over four hours to walk from the north end of the lake to Buttermere village. Inquiries 0870 608 2 608.
Distance:	8½ miles
Terrain:	Many good paths and tracks on the east side of the lake. Some rugged walking over Hause Point. Unbridged streams on the west side, but these are fun to step across using boulders. Boggy patches can generally be avoided but not always – again some boulder hopping might be needed. Generally clear, level paths.
Map:	OS Explorer OL4, The English Lakes – North Western area.
Public toilets:	In the National Park car park behind the Fish Hotel.
Refreshments:	In Buttermere village

The Walk

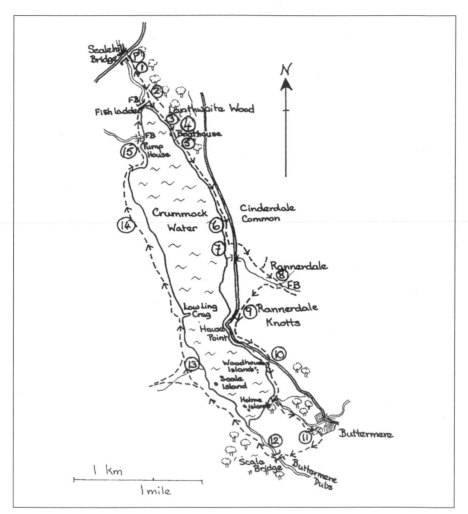

1. Leave the car park by a gate at its end to walk a wide track. Where it divides take the lower one.

Q. Can you name the shrubby plant with pink flowers, growing beside the way?

A. Heather. For about ten months after blossoming the flowers retain their shape and form but the colour gradually fades.

2. **Take the lower track each time the way divides. This brings you to the lake shore, where there are two seats below a huge Scots pine.**

☺ Pause here to enjoy the spectacular view. The whale-shaped mountain to your right (west) is Mellbreak.

3. **Climb the slope left through the trees to join a track, where you continue with the lake to your right.**

☺ Here the floor of the woodland is covered with wood-rush. Its leaves are like the wide blades of short grass, fringed with white silky hairs; the flowers are chestnut brown.

4. **Continue on to a boathouse on the lake shore.**

Q. Look at the notice on the boathouse door. What does the National Trust hope will happen when some of the trees are removed from Boat House Brow?

A. Deciduous trees will regenerate the slopes.

Q. Why does the trust think this will happen?

A. There will be more space and light.

5. **Continue along the shoreside path through tall tees. Then cross two step stiles and a stream and go on with a young plantation to the left.**

☺ Ahead is a stunning view of the mountains around this lovely lake. To your left (west) loom the lower slopes of Grasmoor, a huge mountain often endowed with a cap of mist.

6. **Go through a gate onto bracken slopes. Ignore the stile on your left to the road, and continue to another close to the shore. Go on to the next stile (look for the dog flap) into a pasture called Fletcher Field. Pause on the seat and then cross the footbridge to walk between oaks to a small beach. Beyond climb a narrow path to go over two footbridges, continuing through gorse bushes 8ft (2.5m) tall. Look below the ash trees you pass next for foxgloves.**

☺ Foxgloves have tall purple blossoms often 2 to 4 feet (0.75-1.25m) high. The Latin name for the plant is *Digitalis purpurea*, which means a finger-stall or thimble, accurately describing the shape of the lovely flowers. They have soft downy leaves, which provide pleasing greenery in winter. Some are biennial, producing leaves in the first year and flowers and seeds in the second.

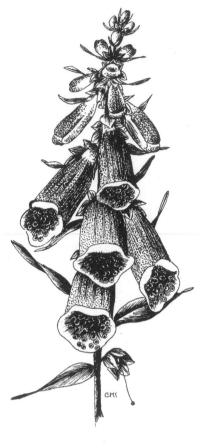

Foxglove

7. At the wall ahead, turn left and walk to the stile to the road. Cross
    with care to the car parking area, opposite, on Cinderdale Common,
    named after the cinders tipped on the fellside by ore smelters. Out of
    the car park leads a signposted track. Head on along this towards the
    small rugged peak ahead, **Rannerdale Knotts**, stepping across
    Cinderdale Beck. Stride the terrace-like path as it leads into the
    peaceful valley of **High Rannerdale**.

☺ It was not always so quiet and tranquil. During an attack by the
    Normans, local Lakelanders encouraged the marauders to think it
    was the only route to Buttermere and trapped them in the valley.
    From the heights on either side the archers soon finished off the
    invaders.

8. Go on to cross a stile. Beyond follow the track as it drops right to cross a footbridge over Rannerdale Beck. Turn right and follow the clear way as it winds around the skirt of the Knotts, with a derelict wall to your right. The track then comes beside an intact wall on the right. Go through the kissing gate and stroll on the lovely way to come to a small parking area beside the road.

Q. What is the small parking area called?

A. A 'dive site' which has to be pre-booked to leave your vehicle there.

9. Walk carefully along the roadside for 50 yards (45m) and then, ignoring the footpath, take the bridleway that leaves on the left. It goes a short way up Hause Point and then swings left. Follow it as it zig-zags to cross the shoulder of the crag.

😊 It is almost impossible to believe that this was once the only route into Buttermere (this would have been the track concealed from the Normans). The horses pulling the carts must have found it hard work. It is said that some people have spotted cartwheel marks on the rocks! Today the metalled road edges the shore, suitable for vehicles but not a place to walk if it can be avoided.

😊 As you descend the other side the view of all the mountains and the islands on the lake is magnificent.

10. At the road side cross with care, and look for the well built steps leading down to a kissing gate which gives access to a permitted footpath. Continue along the lake shore and then swing slightly left across the pasture to another kissing gate. Go on through oak woodland, with the lake beside you. Pass a boat jetty, cross the footbridge and pass through the next stile. Beyond, stride across a delectable beach at the head of the lake. Cross another footbridge, beyond which you turn left. Follow the fence on your left. Ignore the footbridge over Mill Beck and go on along the path, with the beck to your left, to pass through two gates and into the car park behind the Fish Hotel.

11. Turn left, pass the toilets and, once in front of the hotel, swing right to walk a broad track in the direction of the fine waterfall tumbling down Sourmilk Gill (walk 9). Pass through a kissing gate and take the next one on the right, signposted Scale Bridge and Scale Force. The track beyond leads you directly to the bridge which crosses Buttermere Dubs.

Q. How many arches does the bridge have?

A. Two.

Q. Which way does the beck flow?
A. From Buttermere to Crummock Water.

Crummock Water

12. Beyond the bridge follow the track right. It has been well reinforced in places. And then Crummock Water opens out ahead of you. Step across Near Ruddy Beck and then Far Ruddy Beck. Notice as you go the reddish coloured soil and the pinkish boulders. At a large cairn continue on the grassy track, ignoring the rough track that leads up and away left. This is the route taken on walk 11. Go on with Scale Island to the right and pass through a large clump of holly trees. Beyond, the path is indistinct as it strikes slightly left for a short distance to avoid a boggy area. It then continues parallel with the lake. Step across a small stream (a branch of Scale Beck), and then take a wide green track through bracken — it has been visible for some time —to come to the side of Scale Beck.

☺ Upstream of the hurrying brook lies the dramatic waterfall Scale Force, hidden from view in a deep cleft. It is not visited on this walk.

13. Step across the beck or walk left to take the footbridge. Stride on the continuing path, which is not very clear and in places wet. It brings you to Low Ling Crag, an unusual spit of land projecting into the lake, with a craggy outcrop at its end. Just beyond, look left to see, high on the slopes, traces of iron-mining on Mellbreak. Once past Low Ling Crag, keep to the upper path to avoid more marsh.

☺ This side of the lake is very quiet. From it you have some of the finest views in the Lake District. It is a good place from which to spot pochard, cormorants, mallard, geese and tufted ducks. Among the rocks outcropping the shoreline, watch for wheatears, meadow pipits and stonechats. The male stonechat is a conspicuous bird, with a black head, white collar and pinky breast. Look for it perching on top of a boulder or a straggly gorse bush, frequently jerking its tail, calling as it does; its call sounds like two pebbles struck together, giving it its name.

14. Pass through a gap in a ruined wall. From here you can spot the gate beside the lake. Continue through it but do not descend too quickly – stay higher up the fell to avoid another dampish area. Once through the gate, follow the path edging the lake, with a great bank of sweet smelling gorse to your left. Pause again for another grand view of the mountains below which you walked earlier. Go through the next gate and pass a pleasing beach. Climb a small slope and continue between birch and hawthorn, now up above the lake, to go through the next gate.

15. Keep to the path to the left of the concrete edge of the lake to walk round the wire fence about the pump house. Continue edging the lake. Cross the footbridge over Park Beck. Press on along the water's edge, with the lake narrowing all the time to its foot. Cross the foot-bridges over the weirs, where the River Cocker leaves the lake. Go on to the Scots pine where you had your first view of Mellbreak. Turn left, join the track, keeping to the lower one each time it divides, to return to the car park.

11. Scale Force, Crummock Water

Scale Force descends in one continuous drop for over 100ft (30.5m) and because the fall is unbroken it is considered Lakeland's highest fall. It is at its most dramatic after several days of rain. Holly bushes clothe the side of the cleft through which the force hurtles. The trees maintain a hold where any small ledge provides sufficient soil and nutrients. A visit to Scale Force was once a favourite outing for our Victorian great grandparents. They did not go on foot, however, but were taken by rowing boat across the lake from the opposite shore, near Hause Point (struggled over in Walk 10).

Starting point: Car park behind the Fish Hotel, Buttermere. Grid reference 173169

By bus: Cumberland Stagecoach 77, Keswick, Lorton, Buttermere. Summer service only. Inquiries 0870 608 2 608.

Distance: 4 miles

Terrain: Fairly easy walking. The last part of the cairned track is stony. After rain, paths can be wet – but then the waterfall is excellent!

Map: OS Explorer OL4, The English Lakes – North Western area.

Public toilets: In car park

Refreshments: In Buttermere village

The Walk

1.   From the car park return to the entrance and bear round right in front of the hotel. Bear right again and walk on to pass through a gate. Take the next gate on the right, signposted Scale Bridge and Scale Force. The track beyond leads you directly to the bridge across Buttermere Dubs. Stand on the bridge and look for trout swimming between the two lakes.

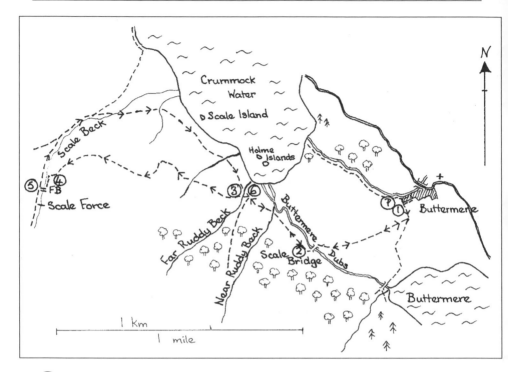

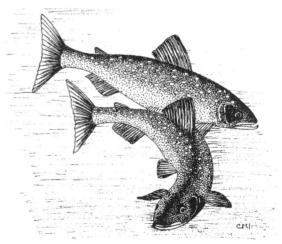

Trout that live in large lakes can grow to 0.6m in length. The food of trout consists of aquatic insects and crustacea. Lake trout also eat plankton and the largest eat fish such as perch, stickle-backs and minnows. Char is another fish that lives in Buttermere and Crummock Water. It is a fish of deep, cold lakes. Unlike trout it has white edges to some of its fins, and has light spots on a

Arctic Char

darker background; trout have dark spots on a lighter ground.

2. Cross the bridge and turn right to follow a good path. Soon Crummock Water opens out ahead. Step across Near Ruddy Beck and then Far Ruddy Beck.

3. At a large cairn, where the path divides, take the upper way, which continues as a wide rough cairned track. The path moves away to the left and then a little to the right as the bouldery way continues below a line of hawthorns. The continuing cairned way goes on. Cross a small stream and more wet ground and then stride a stony path heading for a gap in a wall.

Q. Stand still here and listen. What is the sound?

A. Falling water. You are near to Scale Force.

4. With care scramble over the reddish boulders to see the force. Parents must decide whether children should climb up to see more of the dramatic chasm and will want to accompany their adventurous youngsters. If all the boulders are wet even more care is required to avoid slipping. For a good view and from a

Scale Force, Crummock

safe distance press on down the path, beyond the gap in the wall, to the bridge, over the beck, immediately below the force.

☺ A waterfall can be formed where a river flows from a hard to a less hard rock, the latter is worn down more quickly, and a more or less vertical face is created. At the base of the fall a hollow or plunge pool forms. Other waterfalls result from the action of glaciers. In some areas a glacier scooped out the bottom of a valley. Smaller valleys which led to the main valley became 'hanging valleys' and now streams left high in the hanging valleys plunge downwards in dramatic falls.

5.   Once over the footbridge, turn right and walk downstream to the next footbridge, which you cross for your return. Continue downstream for a few more steps to take a good path heading away from the beck and passing through bracken. Step across another beck. Beyond, the path after rain crosses boggy ground and it is better to climb up right to find a drier way. Go on through a large clump of holly trees and continue to the largish cairn, where you took the higher path on your outward walk.

☺ Everyone can recognise a holly tree, with its dark leathery leaves which generally have spines. Sometimes these are missing from the leaves of the upper branches. Holly leaves burn furiously and the wood itself burns well even when it is green. The trees thrive only in unpolluted air. They can grow in deep shade, such as the great cleft down which Scale Force hurtles.

Q.   Why does little vegetation grow beneath the trees?
A.   Because the holly casts a deep shadow and lowly plants cannot get enough light.

6.   Return by your outward route.

12. Nether How, Crummock Water

This 2-mile walk is just right for very young walkers and for older-ones when the day is too hot for a long trek. Nether How is an oak covered mound from where you can look up the length of Crummock Water.

Starting point: Car park behind the Fish Hotel in the centre of Buttermere village. Grid reference 173169.

By bus: Stagecoach Cumberland, 77, Keswick, Lorton, Buttermere. Inquiries 0870 608 2 608.

Distance: 1 mile. Extended walk 2 miles.

Terrain: Level footpaths

Map: OS Explorer OL4, The English Lakes – North Western area.

Public toilets: In car park

Refreshments: Buttermere village

The Walk

1. Leave the far end of the car park by a gate close to Mill Beck. Pass through a second gate and continue on a narrow footpath. To your right the pleasing stream hurries between its flower-bedecked banks. Ignore the footbridge over the beck and continue on beside a fence to

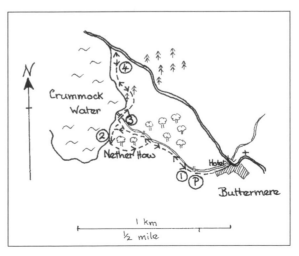

your right to the shore of the lake and the mound of Nether How.

2. **Start to walk round the mound on a clear path. Just beyond a small area of scrambling, take a pause.**

☺ From here, on the south west side of the wooded mound, you can see the low-lying strip between Buttermere and Crummock Water. The two lakes were one – a fact that is easy to believe standing here. This area was formed of debris laid down after the ice-age.

Q. What do think has stabilised this debris?

A. Vegetation.

☺ As you continue round the hillock, you may see a tree creeper climbing the bark of one of the oaks. It looks like a mouse. It has a pointed bill which it pushes into crevices in the trunk of the tree or its branches and with this it extracts insects and spiders. If they are difficult to pick out it will brace itself against the trunk with its feet and stiff tail – it rarely loses the battle. After it has climbed some way up the tree it flies to the next one and starts from the bottom working its way upwards.

3. **To extend the walk after you have returned to the shore, cross a second footbridge over Mill Beck, just before it enters the lake. Follow the shore path, with the lake to your left. Go through a stile and cross another footbridge. Dawdle along the lovely way to pass a small boat jetty and on through more delightful oak woodland. Beyond the next kissing gate the path continues over a pasture to the lakeside and then the road.**

4. **To avoid walking this busy road return by the same route, back through the small wood and along the shore and then, after crossing the second footbridge, turn left to walk beside the beck. Once again ignore the footbridge on your left and continue to the car park.**

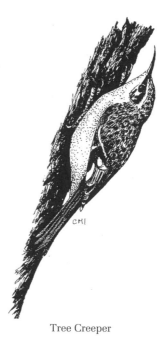

Tree Creeper

13. Loweswater

Loweswater, Crummock Water and Buttermere were once one lake. The last two fill the flat bottom of a steep-sided glacial valley. To the north western end of the valley lies Loweswater and here the hills are rounded and lower. The National Trust owns the lake, together with Holme Wood and two farms Watergate and High Nook. Both of these were built in the 18th century and have fine interiors which include wide staircases, iron fireplaces and shuttered windows. The money to provide such finery is believed to have come from the profits of a lead mine to the east of High Nook Tarn. Above the tiny tarn you can see a zig-zagging track. It is a turbary road – that is, one used for carrying peat. The glorious track above Holme Wood was an old coffin road (or corpse road), where the dead of the valley were carried on horseback to St Bees Abbey for burial. The lake is a haven for birdlife. Look for red-headed pochard, great crested grebe, tufted duck, sandpiper, geese, cormorant and dipper. If you return by the woodland path you might disturb woodcock crouching low beneath the trees.

Starting point: The National Trust's Maggie's Bridge car park. Grid reference 135210. This is marked neither on the OS map nor by the roadside. It is approached by a narrow lane, with few passing places, from the south side of the road that runs beside Loweswater, at its south eastern end. It is very small and soon fills on a summer's day. There is a donation box.

By bus: See walk 11. Nearest bus stop two miles from the starting point, on the B5289.

Distance: Shorter walk 3½ miles. Longer walk 5½ miles.

Terrain: Easy walking but a steep climb up a grassy way above High Nook farm.

Map: OS Explorer OL4, The English Lakes – North Western area.

Public toilets: None

Refreshments: None on walk. Try Buttermere or Lorton.

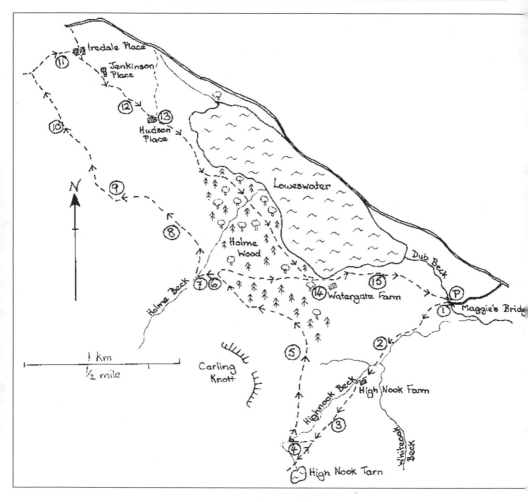

The Walk

1. **From the car park walk back a few yards to take the farm gate, now on your right. Cross the stone bridge over Dubs Beck and walk on in the direction of High Nook farm. Pass through the next gate, with Highnook Beck to your left.**

Q. Look for the hogg-hole on your right at the foot of the wall. What do you think it was built into the wall for?

A. This was to allow young sheep, or hoggs, to pass through the wall, while holding back larger animals.

☺ Look out on your walks for a much smaller hole in a wall. This is known as a 'smoot' and was part of a trap for catching rabbits. It had a concealed trap door on the opposite side and a pit in which to retain the rabbit.

Hogg hole, Loweswater

2. Ignore the ladder-stile on the right and continue on to pass the confluence of Highnook and Whiteoak becks. Follow the track as it passes through a gate to the right of the farmhouse.

3. The track now climbs steeply uphill and young children should be kept away from the edge. Beyond the next gate, where the track branches, keep to the right fork. Look ahead to see a wooden footbridge over the beck. After visiting the delightful tarn you cross this bridge to continue the walk.

☺ Walk ahead to come to the side of High Nook tarn, which sits in a heather covered hollow between Black Crag and Carling Knott. It is fed by a small stream descending from Black Crag and water flows out of the tarn into Highnook Beck. It is the shallowest tarn, at 6ft (1.8m), visited in this book.

4. Return along the path and bear left towards the beck, and cross it by the footbridge seen earlier. Beyond bear right to begin the long climb up the coffin road.

☺ From the path look across the valley to the largest mountain. This is Grasmoor. It shows a fine example of a truncated spur. Once the mountain extended from its summit in a grassy spur towards Crummock Water. Then a glacier, moving along the valley, cut off a large piece of the spur. Watch for the moment when you can see the corner of two lakes.

Q. Can you name the lakes?

A. Loweswater to the left and Crummock Water to the right.

5. Go on along the wide track, now with conifers over the wall to your right and the steep rough slopes of Carling Knott to your left.

☺ Look for the moss named sphagnum on the slopes to your left. This is the moss you have probably already encountered on some of your walks. It can absorb large quantities of water and becomes a spongy mass. Squeeze some and see how much water a tiny handful can hold (unless you are visiting the Lake District in a drought). There are white, red and green sphagnums. They thrive in wet, badly drained and acid places. As the moss has accumulated over the centuries it has produced blanket bog and then peat. In the 1914-18 war it was used in dressings to absorb moisture from war wounds.

6. As you stroll on look for the stile on your right into the forest. This is the point where younger walkers might wish to return. The path beyond the stile excitingly descends, down and down, crossing three wider forest rides, to arrive at the lakeside close to Watergate farm. On this path you might disturb woodcock. Turn right on the main track to leave the forest and follow it through pastures to the car park.

7. To continue on the longer walk, go on downhill to a footbridge over Holme Beck. Look for the small planting of larch on your right.

Q. Why are the larch trees all leaning towards the lake?

A. They receive the full force of the wind that blows down the gill.

8. Beyond the bridge go on along the high level airy way. Children should keep away from the edge at one point. Sit on the ornate seat and enjoy the magnificent view towards Crummock Water.

Q. What is carved on either side of a man's name, on the seat, and on the uprights ?

A. Walking boots. Acorns and oak leaves.

9. Keep on the main track (left branch at the division of ways) and climb to a ladder-stile, and eventually a stile. Go on and on beside the wall to your right. Once past a craggy outcrop on your right climb the ladder-stile over the wall.

10. Continue ahead with a wall to the right.

Sandpiper

☺ Look left over the West Cumbrian plain to the Solway estuary and to Criffel, a large mountain in Scotland. The views to the right are just as dramatic.

11. Continue steadily downhill to pass through a gate and follow a track to a three-armed signpost. Press on in the same direction to walk a very narrow lane to pass a dwelling called Jenkinson Place. Stride on to a stile and gate beyond which you walk a cart track.

Q. Look for the water trough in the hedge on your right. What was it used for?

A. A drinking trough for horses.

12. Take the stile on the left and walk ahead in the same general direction to pass through a gap in the wall. Stride on, with a row of hawthorns to your left, to a stile. Walk on, with a similar hedge still to your left to take a stile on the left to walk around Hudson Place to join a metalled road. Turn right.

Q. What is the datestone on the pretty house?

A. 1741.

13. Follow the rough footpath that bears left in the direction of Holme Wood. Pass through the gate, or climb the stone stepped stile, to join the wide track through deciduous trees. Just after it comes beside the lake, the long footpath through the woodland, mentioned at point 6 above, joins the track.

14. Leave the woodland by a gate and follow the track to Watergate farm.

Q. What is the triangle of holes for, to the right above an archway into a barn. How many holes are there?

A. It is an imitation pigeon loft and there are 13 entry holes.

15. Continue on the gated track to return to the car park.

---

14. Vale of Lorton

The Vale of Lorton is regarded as one of the most delightful valleys in Lakeland. It links the market town of Cockermouth with the high fells of Buttermere, Crummock Water and Loweswater.
The following three walks, of varying length to suit the ages of the youngsters in the family, take you through this lovely area.The return is made along narrow lanes and through quiet pastures.

Starting point: The National Trust's pay-and-display car park north-east of Scalehill Bridge. This is well screened by trees and easy to miss. GR 149215.

By bus: Summer service only. Keswick, Lorton, Buttermere. Cumberland Stagecoach 77. Inquiries 0870 608 2 608.

Distance: Short walk – 2½ miles. Longer walk – 6 miles. Longest walk – 8 miles.

Terrain: Easy walking all the way.

Map: OS Explorer OL4, The English Lakes – north western area.

Public toilets: None

Refreshments: None on walk. The Wheatsheaf pub at Lorton.

The Walk – short one

1.   Leave the car park by a kissing gate at its far end, with the River Cocker hurrying on its way from Crummock Water on your right. Ignore the first left turn and, where the path begins to descend, take the left branch along a shelf-like path above the lake. Emerge from the trees, climb the next stile and beyond turn right to follow the track, which curves left to a gate. Go through it and walk ahead, keeping to the left of the outbuildings of Lanthwaite Green farm.

2.   Once over the stile, cross the road and walk right. A signpost directs your left over the open fell. Cross the footbridge over the Liza Beck which tumbles ecstatically out of Gasgale Gill. (Ignore the footbridge

to the left, that also crosses the Liza) Walk ahead and then bear left to come close to the wall on your left. Continue left with the fell wall still to your left. Above you towers the formidable Whiteside End.

☺ Look over the wall to see vast patches of gorse. Gorse is sometimes named furze or whin. It has dark green rigid spines along its stems; these are leaves and are so shaped to reduce the amount of water lost by the plant. It has highly scented pea-shaped flowers. It blossoms for much of the year and there is an old saying that 'kissing is out of season when the gorse is out of bloom'. In years gone by gorse was crushed and used as winter fodder for animals.

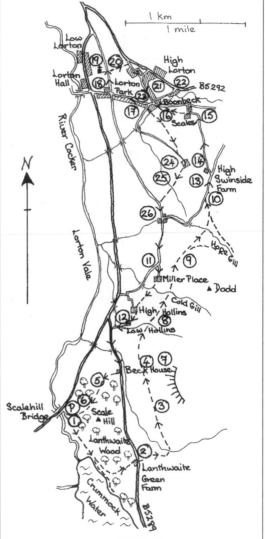

3. Continue along the clear path that passes through bracken, with the wall to the left.

Q. Why is the path grassy with no bracken growing in it?

A. Because it is trodden by walkers and sheep and also grazed by the latter, stopping the growth of plants other than grass and low growing 'weeds'.

Q. Bracken is known as 'Britain's worst weed'. Can you suggest why?

A. It takes over ground where grass and heather flourish, both of which are much more useful to farmers.

4. Continue to the large ladder-stile over the wall, which you climb. Beyond, walk ahead to cross a small stream on convenient boulders. Stride on to cross a footbridge over the Liza Beck to join, with care, the B5289. Cross and pass through the gate opposite, signposted Scalehill. (This is the gate to which you return on all the following routes on this walk.)

5. Follow the lovely path, with a wall to the right. Go through the next gate and walk ahead. Where the woodland ends on the left bear slightly left to climb a clear path through bracken towards the conifer trees on the horizon. At the walled woodland walk left beside it to climb a steep slope. At the top is a stile into Lanthwaite Wood.

6. Carry on along the narrow path, staying parallel with the wall on your right. Take care as it begins to descend and then take the right branch as it descends a little more steeply. Cross through conifers to the forest track seen ahead. Turn right and almost immediately left to descend a path through more conifers to come to the gate to the car park.

Longer Walk

7. Follow the route described above until you reach the ladder-stile, which you ignore. Continue on the clear way above the fell wall. Ahead lies the lovely valley. It is quilted with fields, which are bounded by walls and deciduous hedgerows. Look for the white tower of Lorton church set among trees.

☺ Above on the fell slopes graze Herdwicks, the sheep most commonly associated with Lakeland. They can survive bitter winters unaided. You can recognise the lambs by their black bodies, faces and legs. As they grow they get lighter in colour all over, with white faces and legs. The rams have spiral horns. Herdwicks have a strong hefting, or homing, instinct and rarely stray far from the area of birth.

Q. Why is this instinct important?

A. A useful characteristic in the unenclosed land above you.

8. Continue to pass beside a wall on your right, the lower side of two en-

closed pastures known as intakes into which sheep are taken. Go through a gate and stroll on. Look right to see the tree-lined Cold Gill. The grassy path continues, with the wall to the left and the steep slope of Dodd to your right. Look for the white stones in the wall, which will have come from a vein of quartz nearby.

Q. Why is there extra fencing along the fell wall?

A. To keep the sheep out of the intake pastures. Sheep are excellent jumpers!

9. Continue to Hope Beck, which you cross by convenient stones.

☺ Look for the ruin of a sheep fold and wool washing place used before chemicals and special dipping troughs became available. As you walk, look for the coloured daubs, or smit, on the sheep. Sheep are also given a nick in the ear (a lug mark). Both smit pattern and lug mark are specific to the farm the sheep belong. The patterns and marks are recorded in a book called the 'Shepherd's Guide'.

Q. When would this be most useful?

A. When gathering in the sheep and then trying to identify strays.

10. Continue to a narrow road. Turn left and dawdle to the T-junction Turn left and walk to the next T-junction. Here take the left branch and continue to Miller Place, where the Mellbreak hounds are housed.

Q. What is the date on the farmhouse?

A. 1766

11. Pass through the gate on the right at the end of the dwelling and then, keeping beside the wall on the left, head for a gap stile in the wall. Beyond go on to step over Coldgill Beck and continue. Step across the fences if the stiles are not in place and walk on to a metal gate on your right. Once through stroll on the pleasing fell slope, keeping to the left of the garden wall of a dwelling named High Hollins. Follow the wall round right to a gate onto a walled track. Turn left.

12. Walk the delightful walled track to pass Low Hollins. Stroll on a walled, gated track to join the B5289, where you turn left. Walk with care along the road, which can be busy in summer, to the footpath, on the right side of the road, signposted Scalehill, just beyond Beck House. Follow the return route detailed above in the short walk.

Longest Walk

13. On reaching the narrow road at point 10, above, turn right and walk
    on a few yards to take the signposted track, on the left, to High
    Swinside farm.

14. Keep to the right of the buildings and walk on along a walled track,
    and follow it as it swings right. From now on the glorious track de-
    scends steadily. Here you might see buzzards.

☺ Buzzards are plentiful in the Lake District and this area is a
favourite haunt. Look for a very large bird with rounded wings.
When on the wing a buzzard will sail on uprising air currents, with

Buzzards circling

its motionless wings outstretched and its flight feathers splayed
out. It has a dark brown back and a whitish, boldly-barred, 'vest'.
Its tail is barred with brown and black. It nests on a broad ledge of
a crag or builds a large nest among the branches of a tree.

15. Press on along the track as it bears left and continues to the hamlet of
    Scales. Pass through two gates, with a dwelling to the right, to come to
    a metalled track, where you turn left. Follow the track round right to
    pass another dwelling on the left and go through the hand gate on the
    right.

16. Walk on, with a tiny stream between the path and a hedge, both on
    your left. Follow the indistinct way as it curves right and becomes a
    wide, straight grassy track, with a wall to the left. Go on to pass
    through a kissing gate to a road. Turn left and walk past Boonbeck
    Cottage. Ahead stands the old Jennings brewery, overlooking Boon

Beck. Cross the beck and turn left to read the plaque on the wall of the building

☺ The building is now the village hall and has been named Yew Tree Hall after the tree behind the building. The tree is reputed to be over a thousand years old and was written about in 1803 by William Wordsworth in his poem, 'Yew Trees'. Under this huge tree George Fox the Quaker preached in 1652. At the gathering so many people wanted to hear and see him that they climbed into the branches of the yew and Fox feared that the tree would be damaged. The meeting was kept in order by Cromwell's soldiers who were stationed in Lorton. People differ as to whether the yew tree is the original one or a replacement.

17. **Walk on to pass the post office.**

☺ Lorton village has two settlements, High and Low Lorton, which lie about half-a-mile apart. The River Cocker flows along the western edge of Lorton. Between 1770 and 1800 the course of the river was diverted to provide a series of weirs and races to power flour and linen mills. As you walk through the village see if you can spot any old mill buildings that have been converted to dwellings.

18. **At the cross roads, bear right to walk beside (on your right) the high wall enclosing Lorton Park. Continue to Lorton church.**

☺ The church, an early 19th century Gothic building, is dedicated to St Cuthbert. It lies midway between High and Low Lorton, set in the middle of the half-mile of fields which separate the two.

19. **Visit the simple, unpretentious church. Look for the kneelers covered with delightful, colourful tapestry work. Peep into the book that relates the story of the kneelers.**

20. **Leave the church, walk right for a few yards. Cross the road to take the signposted grassy trod that leads towards High Lorton. Turn right at the end to walk beside the wall of the Hall. Look for the rare circular smoke-house.**

☺ This was used for smoking fish and ham. It is a battlemented structure and has been recently restored, the repairs being partly paid for by the National Park.

21. **Go on to pass the Methodist chapel.**

Q. What is the date on the plaque?

A. 1840

22. Stroll on past attractive cottages and colourful houses. See if you can spot the forge and the brewery manager's house.

23. Go on to take the left turn to Boonbeck Bridge (crossed as you entered High Lorton). Cross and climb the signposted rickety stile on the right and stride to a stile, just beyond a small stream, in the far left corner. Keep to the left of the 'stranded hedge' and on to another stile in the far left corner. Continue on across the pasture, bearing slightly right to a gate onto a narrow road. Turn left.

24. Pass between the dwellings of Low Swinside.

Q. What is the iron object standing in front of the first building on the right?

A. A water pump.

Q. What is the date on it?

A. 1876

25. Walk on to follow the arrow directing you right on the track to a gate leading to a hedged track. At the end of this, cross the beck on great slabs of stone. Pass through the gate in the right corner of the pasture. Stride ahead to climb a stile set in a small stretch of wall. Step across the beck beyond and head on to pass through a gate, then a wall gap, and on again to a gate to a narrow lane.

26. Turn left and stroll on to cross Hope Beck, ignore the left turn and continue to a Y-junction, where you take the left branch. This leads to Miller Place and the kennels of the Mellbreak hounds. To return to the car park, follow the route directions given for the longer walk – from no 11 on.

Pump, Lorton

15. Spout Force, Whinlatter Pass

The drive along the road that climbs towards the pass makes an interesting start to this walk. Vast plantations of featureless conifers stretch away on either side, but close to the road deciduous trees grow and the vegetation is lush and verdant. The walk to the lovely waterfall is well marked and takes you down through conifers to a secret valley, with only the calls of tits and goldcrests, and the chattering of Whit Beck, to disturb the peace. On your return a short diversion to see Scawgill Bridge and the nearby quarry adds to the pleasure of this excursion before your uphill climb through the tall spruce.

Starting point: A small well signposted car park on the B292. Grid reference 182256. To reach this leave Keswick by the A66 in the direction of Cockermouth. After a mile turn left onto the B292 to Braithwaite village and, continuing on the B-road, follow the signs for Whinlatter Pass. On your way up the pass look for the Whinlatter Forest Park visitor centre, which you may like to visit. Several forest walks emanate from here (leaflet of trails available).

By bus: Cumberland Stagecoach, summer service Keswick – Whinlatter, no 77. Inquiries 0870 608 2 608.

Distance: 2 miles

Terrain: Easy walking. One steep-stepped path.

Map: OS Explorer OL4, The English Lakes – North Western area.

Public toilets: Visitor Centre. Braithwaite village.

Refreshments: Café at Visitor Centre

The Walk

1. Climb the stile out of the parking area into a pasture. Follow the yellow-banded waymarker posts. Look left to see Lorton village lying in its valley below gentle hills (see walk 14) Follow the path as it winds left, with the fence to the right.

☺ Beyond the fence conifers descend steeply, obscuring the narrow gill below. Beyond the gill more conifers, Darling Gill plantation, stretch up and up.

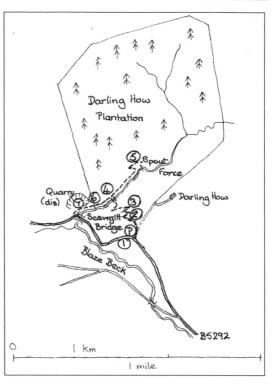

2. Climb the stile into the forest.

Q. Why are the steps of the stile deeply grooved but those of the previous one are not?

A. To stop you slipping as you climb over. As this stile is overhung with trees it takes longer to dry out after rain.

3. Descend the stepped way down and down through the sweet smelling spruce trees, the yellow paint blobs on the bark, as well as the steps, acting as a guide. At the bottom of the steps the path emerges from the trees and continues to a footbridge over the beck, beyond which you turn right.

4. Follow the pleasing path beside the dancing water. Climb the steps left, leading up through the trees. Watch out for your first glimpse of the waterfall. Take care as you walk the path to the railed viewing area.

☺ The beck flows quite leisurely to the edge of the precipice and then leaps tempestuously into the yawning chasm. At first it cascades and then drops in a very long wide curtain of white water into a seething pool almost hidden by a wall of rock. Several ash trees stand at the head of the fall. All are heavily garlanded with moss, lichen and ladder ferns. Great banks of liverworts luxuriate in the constant spray from the outermost streamers of water that ricochet off the confining sides of the ravine.

5. **Return to the foot-bridge. Do not cross but continue down the delightful path — surely a place for a picnic. Look for the wall on your right.**

☺ This is built on a steep gradient — perhaps the steepest site for a wall you will spot in Lakeland — and is constructed of very thin horizontal slabs of stone to provide the necessary strength. In the 19th century a wall 4½ feet (1.4m) high with two layers of 'throughs' would have cost 8 shillings (40p) for 7 yards (6.3m). The stonewaller would have needed about 10 tons of stone. Today the same type and length of wall would cost hundreds of pounds.

Spout Force

6. **Continue on to the gate to the road.**

Q. Look left to see Scawgill Bridge. How many arches has it and where do you think the stone came from?

A. Three arches. The quarry to your right.

7. **Return back along the path to the footbridge, which you cross. Climb up through the trees and follow the waymarks back to the car park.**

16. Forest trails and the Dodd summit trail, Thornthwaite Forest, Bassenthwaite Lake

Whichever trail you decide to follow through this pleasing forest will reveal fine views, and fine trees. The forest roads, tracks and paths are well maintained and easy to walk. The routes are unobtrusively waymarked with different colour bands on posts. Choose the length of walk to suit the ability of the family, then let the youngsters spot the marker posts and lead the way. Directions for a circular route to the summit, 1612ft (502m), are given below and this walk is suitable for energetic near-teenagers. You may wish to buy a leaflet at the tea-room and let the youngsters follow one of the shorter trails or design their own route.

Starting point: Easy-to-miss parking area of Thornthwaite Forest, at the foot of the Dodd, which lies on the A591 just over three miles north of Keswick and on the east side of Bassenthwaite Lake. Grid reference 235282.

By bus: Stagecoach Cumberland bus 555, from Keswick. Inquiries 0870 6082608.

Distance: Short walk – a few hundred metres, Blue Trail – 1½ miles (two hours). The summit of Dodd – 3 miles (three hours).

Terrain: Generally easy walking. The first 550 yards (500m) on the tarmac forest road is a steady climb and then the way eases. Good scramble up a narrow path, through pines, to the summit.

Map: OS Explorer OL4, The English Lakes – North Western area.

Public toilets: In car park

Refreshments: The Old Sawmill Tea-room in car park

The Walk

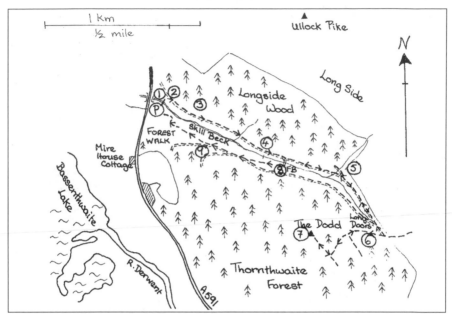

1. **From the car park return to the information boards opposite the saw-mill tea-room. Start the route to the summit by following the red and blue marker posts. Cross the bridge over the Skill Beck.**

Q. What do you think the stone and metal structure across the stream was built for?

A. It was a weir and it controlled the flow of water to a sawmill, now the tea-room. The water provided power to drive machinery.

☺ The large oaks through which you pass are native to this area. Much of the fells and valleys were still covered with natural woodland when the Norse settlers arrived in the 9th century. The name 'thwaite' (Thornthwaite) is Norse for 'a clearing'. By Elizabethan times much land had been cleared of trees so that it could be used for farming and to provide timber for charcoal to smelt ores from the local mines.

2. **Turn right following the red and blue markers and in a dozen yards (10m) turn right onto the forest road.**

☺ Notice as you go some very large
conifers. These are silver firs and
their timber is used for match stalks,
packing cases and carpentry. Resin
removed from blisters on the bark of
young trees is used in mounting
microscope specimens.

Q. The conifers at the start of the walk
are very tall. As you climb those of
the same species and same age
are not so tall. Can you suggest a
reason for this?

A. They are exposed to the wind,
which increases as you climb, and
this checks their growth.

3. As you go on, the red and blue trail
goes off left. The summit trail continues, slightly less steeply, uphill.

Douglas fir cone

☺ Watch out for another large conifer,
the Douglas Fir named after David Douglas who, in 1827, sent the
first seed home to Britain from British Columbia. It grows naturally
on the western side of North America, from British Columbia to
California. See if you can find one of its distinctive cones; it is
egg-shaped and outside every scale there is a straight
three-pointed bract.

4. The marker posts now have only one band, a green one, on them. (Notice where the blue trail descends to the road, on your left. It then
crosses the road and goes on downhill to a footbridge over the Skill
Beck. On your descent from the summit, the circular walk described
here leaves the road and returns by this blue trail, heading down to
the footbridge.)

5. The trees on your left are soon left behind and are replaced by the
austere heather-clad slopes of Longside. Join a forest road coming in
on your left and walk on to take the second right fork, clearly labelled
Dodd summit. Go on climbing and as you turn the corner expect a
dramatic surprise.

Q. Can you name the town, the two villages and the lake that you
can see?

A. Keswick; Portinscale and Braithwaite; Derwent Water.

6. Continue along the level track, with the spectacular view to your left (wonderful if the fells are covered with snow). At a signpost, turn right as directed for Dodd summit and climb a narrow path. An occasional waymarker post keeps you on route to the top of the hill. On the small summit is a cairn with a plaque.

Q. What date is on the plaque and what group did the two people, commemorated on it belong to?

A. 1980; Scouts.

7. Follow the marker post and approach with care the far side of the summit to see another breath-taking view.

Q. What lake lies below and what other country can you see?

A. Bassenthwaite Lake; Scotland

8. Return along the green trail and leave it by the blue path, now on your left, which leads to the footbridge. (See 4.) Beyond the footbridge walk the tunnel formed by the graceful branches of European larch. This lovely path soon joins a forest track, where you turn right and begin your descent towards the car park.

9. At the signpost, turn right for the tea-room, or take a narrow path which brings you back to the car park and toilets.

17. St Bega's church, Bassenthwaite Lake

This short pleasing walk starts from the car park at the foot of The Dodd, a shapely hill belonging to the Skiddaw range, clad in mixed woodland, mainly coniferous. Once it would have been forested by deciduous trees but over the centuries these were cleared and the slopes left bare. In the late 18th century Thomas Storey, the owner of Mirehouse, behind which the walk continues, planted the slopes with trees. Many of these were felled for use in the 1914-18 war. During the 1920s the slopes were replanted with serried ranks of conifers in straight-edged compartments. In the last 20 years or so the Forestry Commission (now Forest Enterprise), who leased the woodland from the Mirehouse estate, brought in a landscape artist to design a forest with less unsympathetic edges, to vary the species and to blend it into the landscape.

The church of St Bega lies on the route. It once served wayfarers and many of today's tourists visit it. The return is over quiet pastures and then by a path through the edge of the forest to the car park. A diversion, by footpaths and a leafy lane, can be made to a small beach on the side of Bassenthwaite Lake.

Starting point: As for walk 16. Grid reference 235282.

By bus: See walk 16

Distance: 2 miles or 4½ miles if a diversion is made to the lake shore.

Terrain: Easy, mainly level walking.

Map: OS Explorer OL4, The English Lakes – North Western area.

Public toilets: In the car park.

Refreshments: The Old Sawmill Tea-room in the car park.

NB: If you wish to visit Mirehouse to view its treasures, walk where the poet Alfred Lord Tennyson walked by the lake, and Excalibur was flung into the water, obtain your entrance tickets from the tea-room in the car park.

The Walk

1. **From the car park, cross the A591 and walk left for 50 yards (45m) and take the signposted footpath on the right. Stride ahead along the hedged track.**

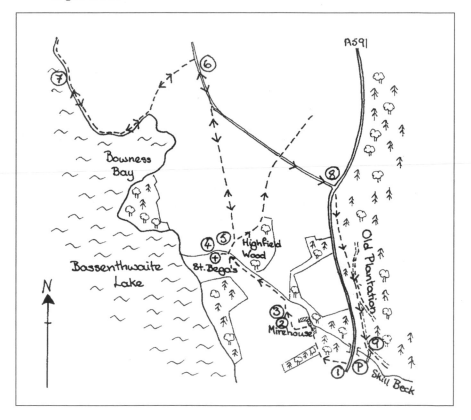

Q. What tree has been used for the hedge?

A. Beech. It provides a good wind break but tends to spread widely and make too thick a boundary – not a problem here.

2. **Follow the track, now edged by yew and holly, as it swings left.**

☺ From here you can see Mirehouse, a 17th-century manor house, where Tennyson was a frequent visitor. He drew inspiration from Bassenthwaite Lake for the passing of King Arthur in his epic poem, Idylls of the King.

3. **Just before the small beck, bear left.**

Q. What has the restored agricultural implement, beside the footpath, been used for?

A. Turning hay.

Q. What are the long 'arms' used for?

A. The long arms are shafts to attach a horse to the hay turner.

4. **Go on to pass through a gate and continue. Stroll on to visit the small, beautifully maintained church.**

☺ The church is dedicated to St Bega. She was the daughter of a seventh-cent

Hay turner

ury Irish chieftain. He wanted her to marry the son of the King of Norway but she had long wished to devote herself to her faith. She fled Ireland and landed at St Bees where she set up a convent. Later she is believed to have lived at Bassenthwaite.

Q. Before you leave the churchyard, walk round it. What shape is it?

A. Round, an unusual shape.

5. **Return the few yards to the main track. If you wish to divert and visit the well signposted way to the lake shore, turn left to stride across the pasture to a stile. Beyond pass through a deciduous copse. Go on in**

the same direction across another pasture to pass through a small wood. Cross two more fields, a track and another pasture, bearing steadily right to join a narrow lane. Turn left.

6.   Stroll on to take a signposted path on the left. (If Bassenthwaite Lake is very high the path will be flooded and you will have to return.) The stiled way takes you beside the reed beds of Bowness Bay and to the lake shore. This might be your choice of picnic site.

☺ Part of the lake is 50ft (15m) deep. It is fed by the River Derwent, flowing out of Derwent Water. The land between Bassenthwaite Lake and Derwent Water is flat, cut through with streams and ditches (seen clearly from the summit of the Dodd on walk 16).

Q.   How many lakes were there once in this valley?

A.   One, until after the last glacier when soil and rock were left behind, creating the small stretch of land, which separates the two present-day lakes.

7.   Return by the same route to the track by St Bega's church. Turn left to walk along the side of the scattered oaks of Highfield Wood. Follow the good track all the way to the narrow road, where you turn right.

8.   At the T-junction turn right and, remaining on the same side of the road, walk on a few yards to arrive opposite a lay-by. Cross with extreme care. Walk to the far end of the lay-by and climb the bank to join a narrow path. This takes you through Old Plantation, keeping parallel with the busy road.

9.   As you near the car park, cross a lay-by and walk a short distance up a forest road. Take the narrow right turn into trees, following a marker post with yellow and blue bands to rejoin your car.

18. Catbells overlooking Derwent Water

Catbells is everyone's favourite. It is shapely, looks easy to climb and has fine grassy slopes. The views from its summit are stunning with, on the right, a glimpse into the Newlands valley and, on the left, the shimmering water of Derwent Water.
Children will enjoy the climb – their first real hill. But though its looks a carefree stroll care should be taken when scrambling is required; and however inviting Catbells looks all the family should use the correct footwear and carry waterproofs.

Starting point: A small parking area two hundred yards along the narrow lane signposted Skelgill, two miles south of Portinscale, above the north-west shore of Derwent Water. Grid reference 247212.

By bus: No suitable buses but Keswick Launch from Keswick Landing Stages on Derwent Water makes frequent calls at Hawes End landing. A short walk takes you to the foot of Catbells. Inquiries 017687 72263.

Distance: From landing stage, 4½ miles. From car park, 3½ miles. Escape routes, 2 miles and 3 miles.

Terrain: Generally easy walking but some grassy slopes are steep. Just one small scramble required.

Map: OS Explorer OL4, The English Lakes – North Western area.

Refreshments and toilets: At landing stage, Keswick

1. Leave by the pleasingly reinforced path that climbs out of the parking area through heather and bracken. From the landing stage, follow the track through the trees to the road, bear left and, where the road makes a U-turn, climb the reinforced track uphill. Follow the zig-zags up the grassy slope, with ever more glorious views as you climb.

Q. Can you name the two lakes that you glimpse as you ascend?
A. Derwent Water and Bassenthwaite Lake

Catbells

☺ Otterbield Island is the smaller one nearest to the foot of Catbells. St Herbert's Island is the larger island just beyond. This is the island visited in one of Beatrix Potter's books. Squirrel Nutkin and his friends visit the island in nutshell boats, with leaves for sails.

2. After reaching the first 'hump' continue on to the second. This requires some careful scrambling. The best way through the crags is up the middle. Look for the plaque set in the face of one large outcrop.

Q. What is the name of the man to whom the plaque is dedicated?

A. Thomas Arthur Leonard

3. Stroll the gently undulating way and go on upwards to the next hummock. Beyond are two small depressions with the final ascent of Catbells ahead. If the family group is young and the ascent is too daunting then take the green path or, a few metres on, the gravelly path, both descending towards the lake. Continue downhill almost to the road to take a delightful track on the left. A seat here is ideal for a picnic.

4. For older children, the last rocky stairway to the summit, at 1250ft (451m) gives them an exciting first taste of climbing a small mountain.

☺ The views from the summit are tremendous. You can see Skiddaw, Blencathra, the Jaws of Borrowdale, Hindscarth, Robinson, Sail and Grasmoor. This great circle of mountains

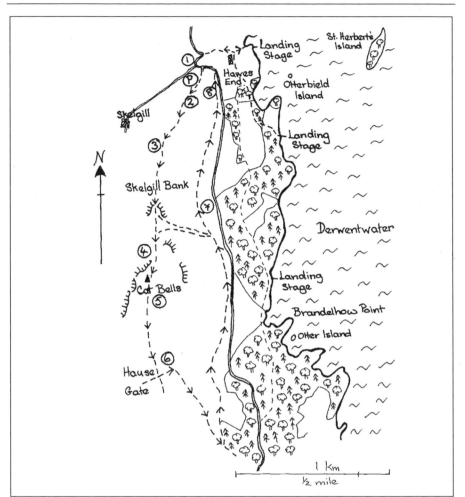

keeps the clouds on the move and makes the light-effects over the lake pleasing to painters and photographers.

5. **Dawdle awhile to enjoy the rocky summit of this lovely hill and then continue along the ridge, an airy highway, to Hause Gate, which is marked by a small cairn.**

Q. There is no gate here. What do you think the word 'gate' and 'hause' means?

A. A way through, or opening between, hills – a pass.

6. Descend left from the Hause towards the lake. The clear path is at first a little steep and slippery, but soon becomes railed and easy to walk. Pass through heather and then bracken to come close to a walled plantation. Here turn left and walk the good track, an old green road used before the metalled road, lower down, was constructed. Very soon the seat mentioned in 3 above is reached.

7. Continue on the glorious terraced track below the skirts of Catbells. Look for gorse bushes that thrive in a large clump by the way.

Q. A small path climbs up the slope on the left. At its foot the National Trust has constructed a fence. Why is this?

A. The fence is to stop you using the path and so to control erosion of the route.

Q. Has it worked?

A. Yes. From the track you can see that vegetation has grown back on both sides of a now very narrow path.

8. Continue along the track to the road. Walk on with care in the same direction. (This can be busy with vehicles in the summer, especially at weekends.) Follow the road as it winds round left and then ignore it where it swings right, continuing ahead to rejoin your car. If returning to the landing stage follow the road as it swings right and then turn right again to pass through trees.

19. Keswick Railway

The Cockermouth, Keswick and Penrith railway line was last used by trains in 1972. The trackbed crosses and recrosses the meandering River Greta, using 'bowstring' steel bridges. The footpath is four miles in length and provides walkers and cyclists with grand views of the surrounding mountains, woodlands and pastures. Much of the footpath is suitable for pushchair and wheelchair users. It was created as a footpath in the 1980s by the Lake District National Park Authority, which continues to improve access. Several fine walks lead off the track, through Brundholme Woods and to Castlerigg Stone Circle.

Starting point: Keswick old railway station next to the Leisure Centre. Grid reference 270237. There are several parking bays in front of the remaining platform. Follow the signs for the Leisure Centre as you drive through the town.

By bus: Stagecoach Cumberland Lakeslink 555/6, Lancaster, Keswick, Carlisle. Inquiries 0870 608 2 608.

Distance: Entire return route on railway track only, 8 miles. Pushchair and wheelchair section, 4 miles. Railway and woodland walk, just over 3 miles.

Terrain: Railway generally flat except for the climb up and down from the top of the Big Tunnel. Woodland path climbs high up through the trees; families need to remind children to walk with care.

Map: OS Explorer OL4, The English Lakes – North Western area.

Public toilets: On the old platform of Keswick station

Refreshments: None on route but snacks can be obtained from the Leisure Centre and in Keswick.

Pushchairs: Suitable from Low Briery or Brundholme to the A66, return.

The Walk

1. **From the end of the old platform, walk ahead along the tree-lined track to stand on a long bridge spanning a fine gorge.**

☺ Through the gorge flows the River Greta, racing over its boulder-strewn bed. The bridge is an inverted 'bowstring' constructed of steel girders; there are more of such bridges to cross on your walk, including upright bowstrings, so restrain your curiosity until you can enjoy viewing them with safety. From the bridge, look right to see some high mountains. These are part of a semi-circle known as the Coledale Horseshoe. To the left are the forested slopes of Latrigg fell.

2. **Walk on the hedged way. Below your feet is the 'Big Tunnel'.**

☺ This place is where trains emerged from the 'Big Tunnel'. It was filled in when the A66 bridge was constructed. During the Industrial Revolution and most of the 19th century the iron ore mines of West Cumberland were expanding rapidly. Although coal was mined locally it was not suitable for use in smelting. So most of the iron ore was sent by train on a circuitous route via Carlisle to the blast furnaces of north-east England. The trains returned with coke from the Durham coalfields to fire the growing number of furnaces. A new railway was desperately needed to provide a more direct, shorter route between the east and

Underslung bridge, Keswick railway

west coast. And so this railway was built. It was completed in 1864.

🙂 To your left, hidden snugly in a tree-girt hollow, is a small hamlet named Brigham. In past centuries you would have seen several mills here, all powered by the fast-flowing River Greta. The woodlands around provided charcoal for early smelting. By the 18th century the mills were producing cotton, wool and felt.

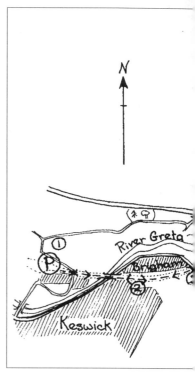

Q. How can you recognise a tree that provided wood for charcoal?

A. It has six or seven trunks coming straight up out of the soil instead of the usual one. These were coppiced. This meant they were cut down to just above ground level. Then the tree grew several poles instead of one trunk. The poles were harvested every 18 to 23 years and the whole process was then repeated. Trees used for charcoal were ash, lime, sycamore, alder and birch. As you walk keep a look-out for trees showing signs of coppicing.

3. **Stride on to pass through a kissing gate.**

Q. What is the name given to the bridge carrying the road overhead?

A. Viaduct.

4. **Follow the waymarks that direct you along a delightful high-level wooden walkway that projects over the tumbling river, first looking back to see more of the hills that form the Coledale Horseshoe. The highest is called Grisedale Pike and the dip to its left is named Coledale Hause.**

5. **Walk on, with the great bulk of Blencathra ahead, to the old platform of Old Briery, now a holiday village.**

🙂 There was a bobbin mill here. In a good year it produced 40 million

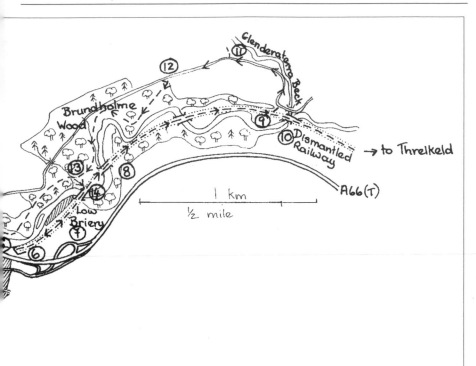

bobbins. Some of these were used in making the coronation gown for the Queen; for producing silk, cotton and Irish linen; and for inserting the metal strip into old pound notes. Bobbins were sent to places as far apart as Uruguay, South Africa and Hong Kong. Pencils were produced in another mill and there was a specialised textile mill, known locally as the 'fancy bottoms mill'.

Q. What do you think this name referred to?

A. Decorative edgings for the bottoms of waistcoats.

☺ The Low Briery bobbin mill closed in 1961. Today Low Briery is an access point for pushchair and wheelchair users. It is a set-down point but it is not possible to leave a car here.

6. Continue along the delightful track and as you cross each bridge decide whether it is an inverted or upright bowstring. Look down on the river below.

Q. Does the Greta flow faster on the outside or inside of bends? Why is there a build-up of stone on the inside?

A. Outside. Build-up caused by the slower flow.

7. **Stroll on until you reach a small stone hut on your right.**

☺ Opposite is a gate which gives another access point for pushchair and wheelchair users after parking on the near-by narrow lane.

8. **To continue on the circular walk, pass through the gate and follow the path to the lane. Bear slightly left and then take your time as you climb the very steep hill.**

☺ The river that flows through the deep gill on your right is the Glenderaterra.

9. **Follow the lane as it swings left. Enjoy the views as you go.**

10. **At the start of Brundholme Woods, look for the signposted path on the left. Walk left on the path and then go with it as it almost immediately swings right. Stroll on this narrow path to a three-armed signpost where you go ahead in the direction of Keswick. Here the path climbs steadily and stays high above the River Greta. The woodland slopes down steeply so take great care. Descend the steps to cross a sturdy footbridge and then walk the clear way until you reach the next three-armed signpost.**

Q. What is the most common tree in the woodland?

A. Oak

☺ The two main species of oak seen in woodlands are sessile and pedunculate. Sessile has long-stalked leaves and unstalked acorns. Pedunculate has unstalked leaves and stalked acorns.

Q. What type of oak predominates in Brundholme Woods?

A. Sessile.

11. **At the signpost, turn acute left to stroll back in the direction you have walked but on a path that drops steadily at first and then quite steeply to the riverside. Climb the steps onto the railway footpath again.**

12. **Turn right to pass Low Briery and saunter on to retrace your outward route.**

Sessile Oak

20. Keswick, Friar's Crag, Castlerigg, Castlehead Wood, Cockshot Wood

This excellent walk over good paths is very popular at the height of the holiday season. Try to walk it at a less busy time. It takes you to the famous Friar's Crag, from where you have one of the loveliest of views. It goes on beside Derwent Water, passing delectable bays where everyone of the family will want to dawdle. It continues, climbing steadily through the mixed woodland of Great Wood below towering Walla Crag. The return is along a path high above the dancing beck that races between wooded banks in Springs Wood. Castlehead Wood with its wonderful view, comes next and, finally, a pleasing path through Cockshot Wood brings you back to the lakeside.

Starting point: The pay and display car park close to the landing stages at the north end of Derwent Water. GR 265229. Leave the centre of Keswick by the Borrowdale Road, B5289, and at the mini-roundabout (on the outskirts of the town), turn right to drive towards the lake. The large car park is well signposted.

By bus: Not required. The walk can be started from the town.

Distance: 4-5 miles

Terrain: Easy walking.

Map: OS Explorer OL4, The English Lakes – North Western area.

Public toilets: In car park and opposite landing stages in Cockshot Wood

Refreshments: In Keswick. At the booking office for the boats. At tea-rooms near to the landing stages.

The Walk

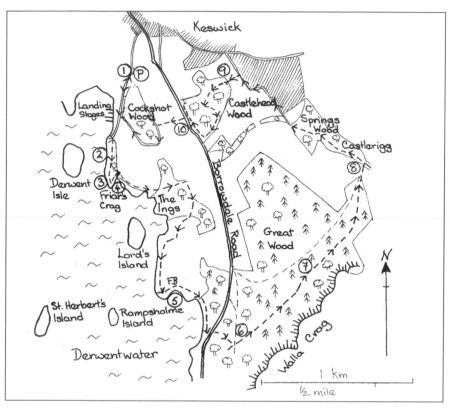

1. Turn left out of the car park and walk the 'no through road' to pass the landing stages on the right and Cockshot Wood on the left. There are picnic tables here on the lake shore. At the road end take the sign-posted footpath to continue on to Friar's Crag. As you go look for the plaque set among the trees.

Q. Who is it dedicated to and why is he famous?

A. Canon Hardwicke Drummond Rawnsley. He was a founder of the National Trust (NT).

☺ He lived from 1851 to 1920 and, with his two friends, Octavia Hill and Robert Hunter, campaigned to preserve the countryside. They worked hard to acquire money to buy land for everyone to enjoy places of natural beauty or of great historic interest. In 1895

The National Trust for Places of Historic Interest and Natural Beauty came into existence. Friar's Crag belongs to the NT and so does the viewpoint on Castlehead. Much of the lake shore and the islands on the lake also belong to the NT.

2. **Go on along the path, through the trees, with the lake to your right. Look for a large slab of slate.**

☺ This is a memorial to John Ruskin, whose head and shoulders are depicted on a copper oval.

Ruskin Memorial

Q. What does MDCCCXIX and MDCCCC stand for?

A. 1819 and 1900, the year that Ruskin was born and the year he died.

☺ Ruskin was a 19th century writer and art critic. He was devoted to preserving the beauty of the Lake District.

Q. What was his earliest memory?

A. The time his nurse brought him to Friar's Crag as a small boy.

3. **Continue to the end of the crag to look over the lovely lake.**

☺ Ahead you can see its shores, almost entirely fringed with woodland. To the right stretches the delightfully named Cat Bells (walk 18) and to the left Walla Crag. See if you can pick out the

Lodore Falls streaming down the hillside. The foot of the valley appears blocked by towering wooded crags. These are known as the Jaws of Borrowdale.

Q. How many islands can you see?

A. Four. There are several very small ones, barely more than a rock. Look them up on the map.

☺ Derwent Isle is the nearest. In the 18th century, Joseph Pocklington, an eccentric, lived there and organised regattas, which included a mock sea battle. Further along the lake you can see Lord's Isle; here lived Lord Derwentwater, a Jacobite, who was beheaded at Tower Hill, London. Beyond lies Rampsholme Island and west of it is St Herbert's Island, the home of the saint in the 7th century. Friars Crag is supposed to be named after the friars who waited for a boat here to take them across to visit the hermit. St Herbert's is also the island that Squirrel Nutkin visited in Beatrix Potter's book of the same name.

4. **Return along the path and bear right, down steps, to a gate on the right, to continue along the lake shore. Follow the waymarked path as it swings inland to enter Ings Wood. Stroll on, cross a footbridge and continue, to emerge from the trees by a gate, where you turn right. Waymarks direct you back to the shore of Calf Close Bay. The delightful path then enters more woodland and you pass through a yew copse.**

☺ The needles of the yew tree are black-green in hue. The trunk is much divided and has thin red-brown bark. The branches of the tree sweep far out and down. Only one seed is formed by each flower; it has a hard coat and is surrounded by a bright layer of red flesh, which attracts birds. Many yews were planted in medieval times because strong long-bows could be made with the wood. They were planted in churchyards to prevent farm animals reaching them because all parts of the tree are poisonous to cattle.

Yew

Q. Why do you think the ground under the yews is bare of vegetation?

A. Plants need, among other things, light to make food and grow. Yew casts a dense shade and ground plants receive insufficient light to thrive.

5. Leave the trees and walk along the shore. Look for the sculpture consisting of a glacial boulder that has been split in two, with each exposed surface carved. The sculpture, placed there in 1995, commemorates the centenary of the National Trust in the Lake District. Just beyond, walk away from the lake to pass through a gap stile to cross, with care, Borrowdale Road. Go through the gap stile opposite and walk right, parallel with the road. Head up a small slope to a parking area, with picnic tables, set among the trees of Great Wood.

6. Pass through the gate at the back of the car park, signposted Ashness Bridge and Walla Crag. Bear right and almost immediately left to take the signposted track for Walla Crag via Rakefoot. The way climbs steadily uphill through larch. As it continues to ascend, the slope to the left of the track is very steep and young children should be under control.

7. Eventually the path levels out. At a division of the track, keep to the signposted right fork and continue to emerge from the trees by a stile, which has a sturdy dog gate. From here you can see Bassenthwaite Lake. Go on along the fenced and walled track with, ahead of you, Skiddaw towering over the houses of Keswick.

8. At the edge of a very deep gill, turn left and take the downhill way for Keswick. Follow it as it swings right into the trees and then turn left before the gill again. Descend to pass to the right of Springs farm and join a metalled road. Walk on for a quarter-of-a-mile. Look for the signposted hedged track (easy-to-miss) that goes off left, opposite a house named Wood Close.

9. Take the kissing gate into Castlehead Wood, climb some steps and bear right. Then take a path off left to climb to the small summit, from where there is perhaps the best view of the whole length of Derwent Water. Return to the lower path and continue to a stile to the road. Again, cross with care.

10. Take the signposted footpath opposite that directs you towards the lake. Enter Cockshot Wood, bear left and follow the track round to join the road at the landing stages. Turn right to rejoin your car.

21. Bowder Stone, Derwent Water

All the family will enjoy this walk through the lovely oak woodlands of Borrowdale. The climb up the Bowder Stone is fun, though care is needed at the top. The return is made through the hamlet of Grange and then beside the River Derwent with, hopefully, time left to wander through Rosthwaite.

Start/finish:	National Trust pay-and-display car park, Rosthwaite. Grid reference 258149. There is an overspill parking area in front of the village hall. Rosthwaite is reached by the Borrowdale Road, the B5289, which runs south through the valley, from Keswick, on the east side of Derwent Water.
Distance:	5 miles
Time:	3 hours
Terrain:	Easy walking along good paths. One steepish climb almost at beginning of walk.
Map:	OS Explorer OL4, The English Lakes – North Western area.

Refreshments and toilets: Rosthwaite and Grange-in-Borrowdale.

The Walk

1. Walk left out of the car park to return to the B-road. Bear left, cross the road and take the signposted bridleway for Stonethwaite and Watendlath. Go over the Stonethwaite Beck by a sturdy bridge. At the two-armed signpost stroll left in the direction of Watendlath, to ascend the walled and hedged track.

Q. Notice the causeway footpath. Can you suggest why it is there?

A. Because the small feeder stream floods the track after heavy rain.

2. Leave the trees by the gate and go on up the zig-zagging gated path,

which has been well reinforced. Pause as you go to look back down on the white cottages of Rosthwaite set among walled pastures, with the steep mountain slopes beyond.

3. Look for the path going off left, signposted Keswick and Bowder Stone, which is the way you continue. This takes you along an airy path with bracken fell to the right and oak woodland to the left. Follow the good way as it descends gently through the trees.

☺ Here you might see Swaledale sheep. In winter they nibble the leaves off fallen twigs as well as the grass that thrives between the well spaced trees. Swaledales have black and white faces and speckled legs. They are strong sheep well able to survive the winter snows on the fells.

☺ As you descend look on the wall on the left for large patches of orange lichen. A lichen is an alga and a fungus living together as one; the alga is green and can make the food for the whole organism. The fungus absorbs and holds the water needed. This lichen will grow only where the air is free of pollution.

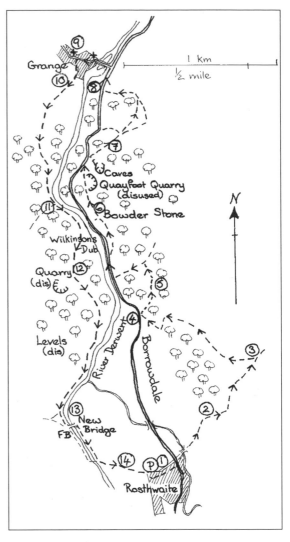

4. **When you can see a gate, ignore it, and head off right to walk a narrow path. Cross a small steam and continue on a green path to pass through a gate. Follow the path beyond as it climbs steadily, and continue where it bears left up a small hillock.**

☺ To the left, on the top of a knoll in a small clearing, stands a solitary wide-spreading yew. Look here for two sides of a small ruined drystone enclosure, close to a huge boulder. This is most likely the remains of a quarryman's shelter.

Q. Why do you think it is a shelter for a workman rather than for sheep?

A. Because the huge boulder, against which the enclosure stands, has been quarried.

Q. What do you think the grassy mounds are at the foot of the boulder?

A. Spoil heaps or heaps of waste slate from quarrying.

☺ Can you find a long groove in a large boulder close by the huge boulder. This would have been made by the quarryman's drill.

5. **Walk on along the narrow path and follow it where it descends to a stile to the road. Beyond, using the path on the other side, walk right for 200 yards (183m) to get past a huge crag that rears up from the**

Bowder Stone

roadside. **Cross back again to take another stile to a track which
leads off in the direction of the Bowder Stone.**

Q. What do you think the oblong slab of slate beside the gate,
with holes drilled in it, was used for?

A. A fence post. Rows of wire passed through the holes.

☺ Climb the wide track to the Bowder Stone. It is fun to climb the
ladder but children should be under supervision at the top. All the
family should take care if the boulder is wet after rain. The Stone is
of Borrowdale volcanic rock, a rock that forms the dramatic
scenery of the Lake District. It is possibly a perched boulder which
may have been loosened by frost and rain and then tumbled from
the slopes above. Or it may have been left where it is by a
retreating glacier. Look up towards the towering crags to see
where it might have come from.

6. **Walk on along the good track to pass Quayfoot quarry to join the
    road.**

☺ Once fine spotted slate was produced here, giving it its other
name, Rainspot Quarry.

7. **Just before the road, the path bears right and joins the access road to
    Quayfoot car park. Bear left through the middle level to a stile over a
    fence (ignore the stile at the back of the car park into the woodland).
    Cross a small beck and carry on to pass another perched boulder.
    The path continues to the right of mounds of quarry waste, almost
    hidden by moss, grass, birch and foxgloves. To the right of the path is
    a small cave, part of the quarry. Press on, keeping to the right of a wet
    area, and, on joining a wider track, turn left to begin your descent
    through woodland towards steps and a stile to the road.**

8. **Cross the road and walk right to Grange Bridge.**

☺ This fine stone bridge over the River Derwent has two arches. It
gives access, in the middle and on both sides, to a small island,
where you might like to have your picnic.

Q. What do you think the square holes are for at the bottom of
both parapets?

A. They are called flood-holes and allow water to escape when
the river is very high.

9. **Continue through the village to come to the church.**

☺ Go inside to see the fine barrel roof of the church, the supports of which have colourful rows of teeth-like projections. Sit on the seat in the churchyard for a short time. You might see and hear nuthatches. These are blue-grey birds with buff coloured chests and chestnut red tail parts. They are difficult to spot as they dart from side to side along branches and tree trunks sometimes up and sometimes down. You are much more likely to hear their loud boy-like whistles and their frequent raps on the bark of a tree when smashing an insect.

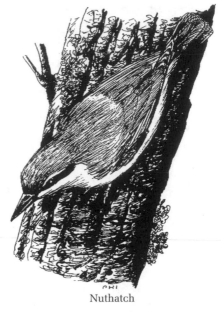

Nuthatch

10. **Return along the road from the church and, in a few steps, take a narrow road, signposted Rosthwaite, on your right. Where** it swings right take a continuing track, which is walled to the left. In the mixed woodland to the right, look for more pitched boulders heavily mantled with moss. Continue ahead to come beside the river.

11. Cross two footbridges over feeder streams and follow the signpost directions for Rosthwaite (yellow arrow) to pass through a gate. Just beyond is a seat overlooking Gowder Dub, a wide shallow part of the river. Press on alongside the Derwent and continue where it swings right.

12. Walk the slated causeway over a wet area that leads to a wall gap, on the left. Beyond, follow the good path to pass through several spoil heaps, almost lost under vegetation. Watch out for the place where the path swings left and then goes on to a kissing gate by which you leave the woodland.

13. Continue on the good track. Cross the cobbled New Bridge over the river and go on towards the village.

☺ Look for the pollarded ash trees to your left. Once the branches were cut off, or pollarded, in the autumn and left on the ground so that sheep could eat the bark during the winter.

14. The track takes you through the buildings of Yew Tree farm and past the Flock Inn tea-room. Bear left to return to the car park.

22. Castlerigg stone circle, St John's-in-the-Vale, Tewet Tarn

This pleasing family walk starts at the famous Castlerigg Circle. It lies two miles from Keswick. The stones, some very bulky, form an oval shape about 30 yards (27.4m) in diameter. Lakeland has several stone circles but this one is unique in having extra stones forming an oblong on one side. The circle stands on a flat pasture surrounded, at a distance, by some of the Lake District's most dramatic fells. The circle is believed to have been put in place during the Stone Age, between BC 2,500 and 1,300. It may have been used as a meeting place for bartering livestock, exchanging partners or celebrating tribal festivals. It may also have been used to calculate the cycle of seasons – vital for farmers.

Starting point: A large lay-by on the opposite side of the road to the access gate to the stone circle. To reach this area leave Keswick by the A5271 and at the foot of Chestnut Hill continue ahead, on the A591, for a very short distance and then take a narrow, well signposted road on the right.

By bus: Cumberland Stagecoach Inquiries 0870 608 2 608. Get off at the bottom of Chestnut Hill and follow the instructions above.

Distance: 4 miles

Terrain: Easy walking, with one steepish climb to the church. Part of the way is over the pastures of Naddle Valley and another section takes you over fell at 1000 feet (305m).

Map: OS Explorer OL4, The English Lakes – North Western area.

Public toilets: None on route. Old railway station, Keswick and in the town.

Refreshments: None on route, but plenty of opportunities in Keswick.

Castlerigg Stone Circle

The Walk

1. **From the lay-by go through the entrance gate to read the information panel.**

Q. Where did the ancient builders of the circle obtain their stone and what geological type was it?

A. They would have obtained the Borrowdale Volcanic series stone from nearby. It was brought here by glacier.

Q. How is it thought the stones were put into position?

A. It is thought they were dragged on log rollers and then levered into prepared holes.

2. **Walk round the site.**

Q. How many stones are there in total and how many in the small 'chamber'?

A. Everyone seems to get a different number.

Q. Two mountains, Skiddaw and Blencathra, overlook the circle. Blencathra is often called Saddleback. Can you decide which is which?

A. Blencathra's ridge, or saddle, looks like one.

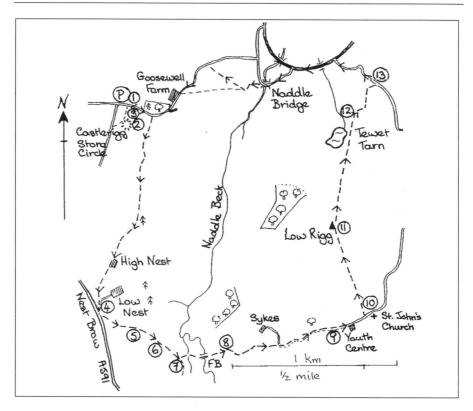

3. Leave the site, turn right and walk for 50 yards (46m) to take the sign-posted footpath on the right. Stride the wide clear way over pastures, to climb three ladder-stiles. Pass through the gate to walk to the right of High Nest. Carry on and, just before the cattle grid, take a gate on the left and descend a short distance, winding round left, with oaks to your right, to a stile onto the access track to Low Nest.

4. Turn right to walk to the A591, where you turn left. After 50 yards take the signposted step stile on the left. Beyond, strike slightly right across a pasture to a gap stile.

☺ Ahead you can see the dramatic Helvellyn range of mountains.

5. Follow the instructions on the wall beyond.

Q. What does the plaque say and why?

A. Please keep near the wall so that you do not damage any crops.

6.   **Follow the wall round.**

Q. What is the tree, with a split trunk and a hole right through it, that grows against the wall? What colour are the buds?

A. It is an ash tree and it has black buds.

7.   **Continue to the gate and beyond go on to cross a tractor bridge to come to a three-armed signpost. Turn left and walk on in the direction of St John's-in-the-Vale church. Follow the waymarked path over the pastures of the Naddle valley to pass to the right of Sykes farmhouse.**

☺ The word Naddle is old Norse for the 'dale of the wedge'. Naddle Fell, immediately ahead, is a long wedge of fell between two valleys.

8.   **Go through the wall, climb the slope and join the narrow rough road to climb its sharp hair-pin bends.**

9.   **Stroll on to come to the Carlisle Diocesan Centre, once a school, and then to the tiny welcoming church.**

☺ It lies snugly under High Rigg and serves both the Naddle valley folk and those of St John's-in-the-Vale.

Q. Look for the war memorial just inside the gate. What is the stone on which the names are carved? What stands next to it and what was it once used for?

A. A huge slab of slate. A sundial. For telling the time of day by the shadows cast by the gnomon on the flat top.

Q. When was the church rebuilt?

A. 1845

☺ Inside the porch there is an information panel which tells you of a well. It is hidden under a tree and it has a cup attached. See if you can find it. Notice the small crenellated church tower.

10. **Cross the road from the church to take the signposted step stile. Head on the grassy swathe through bracken, to a step stile over the wall ahead. Go on, following the arrow, keeping below the hill on your right.**

11. **Do not swing round right below the hill but take a less distinct track continuing ahead, through the bracken. Aim for Tewet Tarn, shortly**

to walk beside a wall on your left. Climb the stile and walk to the right of the lovely pool.

☺ The name Tewet refers to peewits and you will see and hear plenty of these when they are courting and nesting on the pastures around. They are also known as green plovers because of the lovely green sheen of their feathers. Lapwing is another name they are given because of the way they fly. Their call in spring sounds like 'peewit'.

☺ Look for pleasing reflections of Blencathra, in the tarn, as you go.

Lapwing

12. Bear right to climb a gloriously constructed stone stepped stile. Follow the waymarks to walk right, and then left, to pass through a wall gap. Descend the pasture to a gate in the bottom right corner, to join a road.

13. Turn left and walk to the T-junction, where you turn left again. Then turn left once more to cross Naddle Bridge. Climb the stile on the left. Cut across the corner of the pasture to take another. Head left to the wall and then keep up beside the wall on your left, as directed, to join the road again. Walk left to return to the lay-by.

23. Waterfalls in Birkhouse Gill, Thirlmere

The silvery beck that flows through Birkside Gill gathers water from the slopes of High Crag and Dollywagon Pike. It descends its very steep gill under crag-bound trees. At all times of the year water cascades downwards and it brightens the journey for travellers when heading north after crossing Dunmail Raise. The beck then hurries on through the more gentle slopes at the foot of its long fall, eager to join Thirlmere.

Thirlmere reservoir was once two natural lakes, the narrows between crossed by a footbridge. Towards the end of the 19th century, St John's Beck was dammed to create the reservoir. Some years ago, during a drought, divers followed a wall and then a footpath to find the wooden bridge intact beneath the water. The dam at the north end stands 58ft (19.5m) high and 857ft (263m) long and it allowed the water to rise more than 50ft (16m), submerging cottages, farms, an ancient hall and an inn in the village of Wythburn. Daily nearly 50 million gallons (225 million litres) of water flow from Thirlmere into storage reservoirs near Manchester. The attractive, white painted Wythburn Church was not submerged when the valley was flooded. It dates from 1640. It was rebuilt a hundred years later and enlarged in 1872.

Starting point:	The car park behind Wythburn Church. This stands, almost hidden by trees at the south end of Thirlmere on the A591. Grid reference 325136.
By bus:	Stagecoach Cumberland Lakeside Link 555/6. Inquiries 0870 608 2 608.
Distance:	A delightful 2-miler, just right for the very young.
Terrain:	Generally easy walking. Short steepish climb to the forest ride.
Map:	OS Explorer OL5, The English Lakes – North Eastern area.
Public toilets:	None on walk. Nearest at Dobgill car park on the other side of the lake, almost opposite to Wythburn car park.
Refreshments:	Grasmere or Keswick.

The Walk

1. **Continue from the car park to its extension and leave by a gate onto a wide track. Turn right and begin the short climb up through the tall coniferous trees, using the well pitched path (see Walk 26). Climb the stile and turn right to walk a delightful forest ride.**

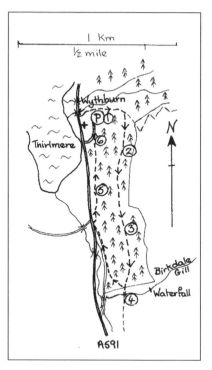

2. **Stroll the pleasing way.**

Q. What do you think the cage-like structure high up on tree, to the left of the path, is for?

A. It is a red squirrel feeder. This is to help maintain the rapidly dwindling population of red squirrels. The reds can get into the feeder and obtain food but not the larger greys, which eat all the food that naturally occurs in the habitat, causing the reds to starve.

Q. If you see a grey squirrel what are you asked to do?

A. Use the telephone number given and explain where you saw it.

3. **Continue on along the high level ride to come to a single plank footbridge. Cross this and stand on the next footbridge.**

Q. How many planks were needed to construct this bridge?

A. Two.

☺ Pause on the bridge to enjoy the series of white-topped cascades. Birkside Beck rises on Dollywaggon Pike and after crossing rather featureless grassy slopes it descends exuberantly through its glorious gill to pass under your feet. Once copper was mined much higher up the gill.

4. **Return from the footbridge to cross the single plank bridge. Ignore the ride you have just walked and take the wide track descending, left, through the trees towards the road. At the road, look ahead and right**

for the small footbridge and then a gate onto a path leading into the trees. The way weaves up and down the gentle slopes and crosses several footbridges.

Q. Why is there chicken wire over the planks of the footbridges?

A. To stop you slipping when the wood is wet after rain.

5. Stroll on, with white arrows guiding you onwards. At a cleared area pause to enjoy the magnificent view of Thirlmere ahead.

6. A short stroll through young conifers brings you to a stile into the entrance road to the parking area.

Red squirrel

☺ Spend a little time sitting in the churchyard. See if you can spot the extension added to the church in 1872.

24. St John's in the Vale

This is a splendid 5½ miler which all the family will enjoy. It takes you through the pleasing Vale of St John's to the small welcoming church that serves the valleys of Naddle and St John's. It continues along a narrow traffic-free lane. The final stretch is below dramatic larch-clad slopes overshadowed by Goat and Iron Crags, and over an unusual bridge.

Starting point: North West Water's car park at Legburthwaite. Grid reference 318195. It lies on the west side of the B5322 very close to its junction with the A591. It is well screened by trees and very easy to miss.

By bus: Stagecoach Cumberland, Lakeslink 555, Carlisle and Keswick to Lancaster. Inquiries 0870 608 2 608.

Distance: 5½ miles

Terrain: Easy walking. One short slope up to church.

Map: OS Explorers OL4 and OL5.

Public toilets: In car park.

Refreshments: Teas available early on the walk at Low Bridge End farm. Keswick or Grasmere. Picnic tables in idyllic setting by the river, over the wall from the car park.

The Walk

1. Leave by a small gate at the far end of the car park to join a narrow traffic-free road. Walk left. Pass through the gate onto the busy A591. Turn right to cross the bridge over St John's Beck and take, immediately on the right, the ladder-stile signposted St John's in the Vale church. Follow the waymarked upper path and, where it soon divides, take the lower (right) fork.

2. Stride on below oaks, high above the hurrying beck, where children should be reminded to walk with care. Follow the lovely way as it begins to descend towards the beck.

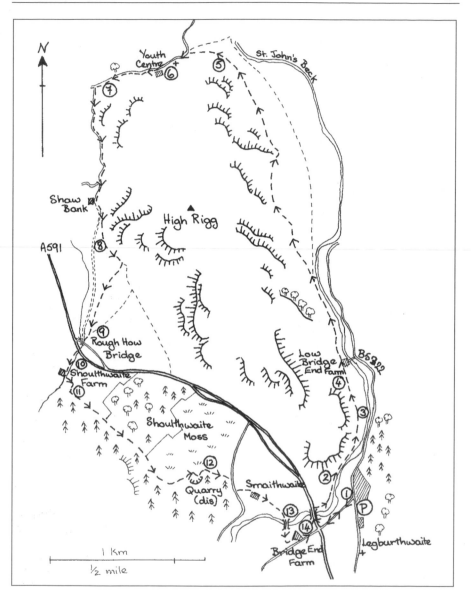

Q. How can you tell that after lots of rain the beck floods its banks?

A. Much debris is to be seen, such as tree branches and dead vegetation lying in a line several feet away from the beck.

3. **Go on below the sheer scree-covered slopes of Wren Crag, where widely scattered ash, larch and rowan grow among lichen-covered outcrops. Look for the pollarded ash trees growing in the pastures on the right of the path.**

☺ When a tree is pollarded its branches are cut back and in the winter sheep eat the bark of the severed branches. The effect of the pollarding is to produce a thick close growth of young branches, forming a rounded head. Cattle that have their horns removed are polled.

☺ Just after you have seen the pollarded ash, and if you are walking in early April, look beside the wall on your right for a tiny green plant with very small yellow flowers. This is moschatel. It is widespread and not at all rare but few people spot it because of its size and apparent dullness. Look closer and you will see it is a wonderful little plant. It has five flowers, four of which have five petals each, and these four flowers face north, south, east and west, just like a clock tower with four faces. The fifth flower turns towards the sky and has four petals.

Moschatel

4. **Just before Low Bridge farm, follow the signpost directing you above the dwelling, the path continuing into larch. Go on along the clear way through a delightful mix of conifers, deciduous trees and areas of open fell. From the latter you have a dramatic view of Blencathra.**

☺ The grand mountain is seen at its best from this walk. Its name is probably Celtic in origin. It has another name, Saddleback, less romantic but apt.

☺ Look right across the valley to see several level mounds below the high crags.

Q. What do you think these levels are?

A. They are great spoil heaps from Bramcrag Quarry, now disused.

5. Stroll on along the pleasing path as it begins to climb gently above Bridge House farm to join a narrow road. Turn left and walk on to the church (visited on walk 22).

Q. Look again at the sundial. Why do you think that the hands of your clock or watch turn in a 'clockwise direction'?

A. It is the direction in which the shadow cast by the gnomon moves as time passes.

6. Turn right as you leave by the gate to pass by the Carlisle Diocesan Centre. It was once a school.

Q. What reminds you of this?

A. The bell high in the eaves.

7. Stride on the narrow road, which zig-zags downhill and then winds left (south). Continue on it below the craggy slopes of High Rigg to your left. Enjoy this traffic-free lane. Ignore the right turn to Naddle and stroll on to pass a house named Shaw Bank. Adjoining it is a dwelling named Ku-Hus.

Q. What do you think Ku-Hus means?

A. Dialect for cow house.

8. Where the metalled road ends saunter on and when the track divides, continue as directed by the signpost beside the wall on your right. Go through the kissing gate to walk on through bracken. Beyond the next kissing gate step onto a narrow road and a bridge.

Q. What is the name of the bridge and when was it built? What do think CCC stands for?

A. Rough How Bridge, built 1904. Cumberland County Council – Cumbria did not exist as a county in 1904.

9. Climb the stone stepped stile on the other side of the road, opposite the kissing gate just passed through, and walk across the small pasture to another stile, beside another bridge. This gives access to the

busy A591. **Cross with immense care and pause in the access track for Shoulthwaite Farm.**

Q. Why do you think there are two roads, both of which you have just crossed?

A. The narrow road, the old bridge and the sturdy stile were part of the old road before the A591 was constructed, with its less than solid stile beside the less sturdy bridge.

10. **Walk up the signposted track and follow it as it bears left.**

☺ Look for the flood control measures along the beck, where cobbles have been used to reinforce the banking.

☺ Ahead you can see two very large conifers. These are Sequoias, the name commemorating a chief of the American Indians. Today Sequoias are amongst the tallest, largest and heaviest trees in the world. The two you can see are Wellingtonias or Big Trees.

11. **Follow the footpath sign directing you between farm buildings to a green metal gate and then another gate into the forest. Continue ahead along the lovely way Look out for red squirrel feeders as you go. After you are three-quarters of a mile beyond the farm you pass an old quarry on the right. Here remain on the track to pass through a gate.**

Q. What do you think the large 'fishing nets', just before the gate, are used for?

A. They are beaters for putting out forest fires.

12. **Beyond the gate turn right. Ignore the stile on the left and walk the track to join a narrow road. Turn right and almost immediately take the signposted footpath on the left. This delightful grassy trod leads to a magnificent barn, its stone covered with orange lichen. Keep to the far side of the barn and continue through the buildings of Smaithwaite. Go through a gate and follow the wall, on your right, to come to a charming bridge over St John's Beck.**

☺ Stand on the ancient arched part which is linked to the pastures on either side by wooden footbridges. Look right to see a small weir, which is all part of the system for controlling the beck when it is in spate. Look left to see a fine row of stepping stones. Once, long before the A591 existed, an old road would have come down to the arched bridge.

Packhorse Bridge, St John's in the Vale – see point 12

13. Beyond the beck, turn left and walk to a kissing gate. Cross a wide track to take another gate.

☺ The track would have been an old drove road along which cattle where driven to a ford beside the stepping stones.

Q. How many stepping stones are there?

A. 18.

14. Walk up beside the wall on your right, towards Bridge End farm and climb the ladder-stile to a narrow road. Turn left to walk to the side of the A591. Cross with great care, pass through the gate and walk the narrow road, taken at the outset of your walk, to pass through the hand gate on the right into the car park.

25. Hesket New Market and Caldbeck

These two lovely fell villages are situated on the very northern edge of the Lake District. They lie at an almost equal distance from Penrith, Keswick, Carlisle, Cockermouth and Wigton and both are easily accessible by car. The villages are surrounded by delightful woodlands and pastures overlooked by the northern fells.

Hesket New Market has a long wide street lined with many 18th century cottages and houses. Down the centre is a pleasing green with a market cross and seats. In winter fell ponies come down from the bleak heights, seeking shelter. The market was established in Hesket in 1751 and there were cattle and sheep fairs in the village until the middle of the 19th century.

Calbeck lies north west of Hesket and once was a busy noisy place with lots of mills, which made use of the water power of Cald Beck (Norse for cold beck) after which the village is named.

Mining in the fells above the two villages started in the 13th century and the mines were at their most successful in the 17th century. Copper, lead and barytes were the main minerals that the miners sought but there were at least another dozen and a half waiting to be wrested from the fells. The last mine closed in the 1960s but for centuries the villages must have resounded to the noise of the clogged miners setting off to work.

Starting point: The car park at the east end of Hesket New Market on the Penrith road. Grid reference 343386.

By bus: No public transport

Distance: 4 miles

Terrain: Easy walking but some paths and tracks can be muddy after rain. For a short distance on two high level paths through woodland overlooking the River Caldew there are steepish drops where children should be under close control.

Map: OS Explorer OL5, The English Lakes – North Eastern area.

Public toilets: In Caldbeck

Refreshments: The Teashop next to the post office and shop in Hesket New Market. Priests Mill, and the Old Smithy gift shop, both in Caldbeck

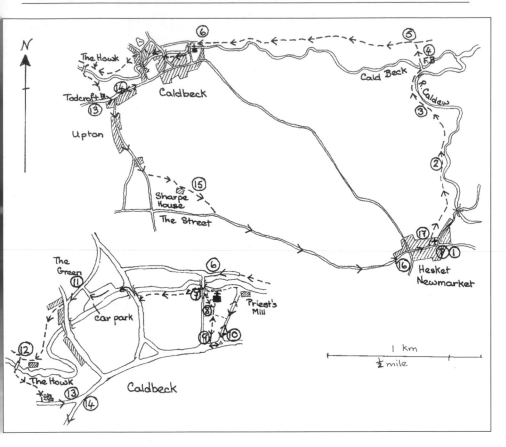

The Walk

1. From the car park, turn left and walk a short way along the main
    street. Cross the road and just before Smithy Cottage take the sign-
    posted footpath on the right. This leads you into an area with swings
    and slides on the left and a picnic table on the right. Walk ahead from
    the stile to cross a footbridge and pass through a gate. Walk right
    along a fenced way and, beyond the next gate, turn left and continue
    high above the pastures that lie beside the River Caldew. Walk on to a
    kissing gate into woodland.

Q. What can you see on the tree to the right of the gate?

A. A bird box.

2. Continue with care along the narrow path through the trees and high

above the river. Emerge from the trees by another kissing gate. Strike slightly left to cross the corner of a large pasture, following several waymarked posts.

3.   Pass through the kissing gate that gives access to another high-level path above the river, where children should be under control. Enjoy this lovely way and then leave the trees by a gate. Follow the path as it winds round right to another stile. Turn left.

😊 Pause here to notice that you now have a river behind you and another in front of you. Just through the trees and out of sight is the junction or confluence of two rivers, the River Caldew and Cald Beck.

4.   Cross the white footbridge and walk ahead and then straight uphill through the rather prickly gorse bushes.

😊 Gorse is often described as a tiresome weed that is highly inflammable. And yet for much of the year it carries enormous trusses of fragrant golden flowers which brighten hedgerows, heaths, fell sides and commons. If when you climb this slope the day is warm, listen for the cracking noise as the ripe pods 'pop' and scatter their polished seeds.

Gorse

5.   Climb the stile over the fence, turn left and walk to the gate into the conifer plantation. Stride the wide track through the trees. Where the way divides keep to the lower path until you come to the side of the Cald Beck. Stride on along a track through a meadow. As you near the houses of Caldbeck village, look through the trees to the other side of the river to see the large waterwheel of Priests Mill.

6.   Turn left to cross the packhorse bridge (rebuilt in 1793) over the beck. Then, with care, descend the steps to St Mungo's Well.

😊 Here a spring made holy by Kentigern, known as Mungo, was used by him to baptise converts in the 6th century, long before the

Church and St Mungo's Well, Caldbeck

church named after him was built. Kentigern came from Strathclyde to preach in Cumbria.

7. **Return up the steps and take the gate on the left into the churchyard. Walk on along the path and continue just beyond the building and look right.**

Q. Whose is the large white marble headstone?

A. John Peel.

☺ John Peel was a huntsman and he lived in the village. He used to wear a grey coat. His good friend, John Woodcock Graves, wrote the words of the song that starts 'D'ye ken John Peel with his coat so grey...'. The writer lived in a house opposite the Oddfellows Arms. The grey cloth was made in the mill he owned.

8. **Just beyond Peel's headstone is one to Mary Harrison (known as the**

Beauty of Buttermere – see walk 9). After you have found her stone you might like to visit the church. It has many treasures and a printed guide to help you interpret them.

9. Leave the churchyard by the main gate and turn left and then left again to visit Priests Mill, where there is a cafe, shops, a museum and of course the waterwheel.

☺ The mill was built by a rector of Caldbeck. From 1702 to 1933 it was used as a stone-grinding cornmill. After that it was a sawmill.

10. Return through the churchyard and, just before the packhorse bridge turn left to take the narrow footpath that leads you to the road. Turn right and cross both Gill Beck and Cald Beck. Pass through the car park on the left and leave by the exit road to come to the side of The Green.

☺ Sit by the pond and enjoy the ducks and geese. Caldbeck Pond is known locally as Claydubs. Once it was a claypit for a brick and tile works. People living around the green have always kept wildfowl on the pond.

11. Bear left along the side of The Green, cross the road and continue ahead along a track signposted The Howk. (The sign is high on the side wall of a barn.) The Howk is a spectacular limestone gorge.

☺ The first building you come to is an open-sided shed for drying coppice wood. Beyond is Mary Bobbin Mill. Built in 1857, it produced bobbins for the cotton industry, clog soles and children's dolls. It had a waterwheel three times as large as the one seen at Priests Mill but it was dismantled and the metal used in the 1939-45 war. A few years ago the mill was a ruin but thanks to English Heritage and the National Park it has been repaired and consolidated.

Q. What is the date on the side of the mill building?
A. 1857, the date that it was built.

12. Climb the steps beyond and pause to look at the vast cavities in the limestone. Once this wall of stone stretched across the beck and was known as Fairy Bridge, but the water has worn it away. Descend the next row of steps and cross the modern day wooden bridge over the cascading water. Go through the stile and bear left round the pasture to pause before the stile to the road.

☺ Look left to see two sets of stones. These are staddle stones. This was once a stackyard and the stones kept the sacks of corn off the ground and away from the rats.

Q. How many stones are there?

A. Two sets, one of five and the other of seven.

☺ Turn left beyond the stile to pass a farmhouse named Todcrofts. Here Mary Harrison (you looked for her headstone in the churchyard) lived happily and raised her family. Previously she lived in Buttermere and had innocently married a villain who was already married. Later he was hanged at Carlisle, not for bigamy but for forgery – a very serious crime in the early 19th century.

☺ Later Mary married the farmer who lived at Todcrofts.

13. **Cross the road and walk on to a picturesque one-up-and-one-down house, now the Old Map Shop. This was once the village school. If you continue for a short distance on the same side of the main road, in the direction of the centre of the village, you might spot the Spit Stone set in a wall in front of a barn.**

☺ For over a hundred years the children of Caldbeck have spat in the stone. It is believed that it once stood on the ground with vinegar in it. Money was placed in it during the plague to pay for food brought in from other areas.

14. **Return to the old school and walk up the lane behind it. Cross the bridge over Gill Beck, ignore the footpath on the left and take the narrow reinforced lane on the left. Beyond the last house on the right, take a signposted way on the left. Ignore the arrowed stile and walk the gated hedged path just before it on your right.**

Q. As you pass the farm on your right look for the gadget with a large handle and a big stone. What do you think it was used for?

A. It is a grindstone used for sharpening cutting implements.

15. **Stride on to the lane, named The Street, and turn left. It is a quiet way but expect the occasional vehicle and walk facing on-coming traffic. The lane leads to Hesket New Market.**

☺ Look for Hesket Hall, a large square house on the left across the road. This was built in such a way that the many corners of the dwelling and the circular roof acted as a sundial and the shadows cast indicated the time of day.

16. **Walk the wide street, passing the teashop and village store on the right, and look for the market cross.**

☺ It has a pyramid-shaped roof and four pillars. It was erected in the 18th century but had to be rebuilt when someone backed a car into it. Look carefully around the outside of the cobbled floor to see if you can find the bull ring.

17. **Walk on along the street to return to the car park.**

26. Lanty's Tarn, Greenside Mine, Glenridding, Ullswater

This glorious walk starts from the car park in Glenridding, a pleasant compact village on the shores of Ullswater. Today the village is geared almost totally to tourism but for three hundred years or so, before the lead mine was closed in 1962, Glenridding was essentially a mining village. Houses and cottages line the main street, which lies at right angles to the lake. The street leads towards the disused mine and is now a bridleway and footpath leading to Helvellyn. This walk returns to the village along this way. Close by is Patterdale Hall, once owned by a member of the Marshall family. He was a relative of the Marshalls of Monk Coniston who created the glorious small Tarn Hows. The Patterdale Marshall dammed Lanty's Tarn to provide (before refrigerators) ice for the Hall. This walk takes you beside the tiny stretch of water, which pleasingly reflects the Scots pine and larch that grow around its banks.

Starting point:	Beckside pay and display car park in the centre of Glenridding village on the west side of the A592 and at the south end of Ullswater Grid reference 386170
By bus:	Stagecoach Cumberland; limited service on the Kirkstone Rambler, number 517. Inquiries: 0870 608 2 608
Distance:	4 miles
Terrain:	Generally easy walking. Steepish climb through woodland out of village. As you approach the mine along a narrow path, children need to be under control.
Map:	OS Explorer OL5, The English Lakes – North Eastern area.
Public toilets:	In car park
Refreshments:	None on route but can be obtained in Glenridding

1. **Return to the A-road, turn right and cross Glenridding Bridge. Turn right again to walk in front of a row of shops on the left and the Glenridding Beck to your right. Pass the public hall and Eagle farm.**

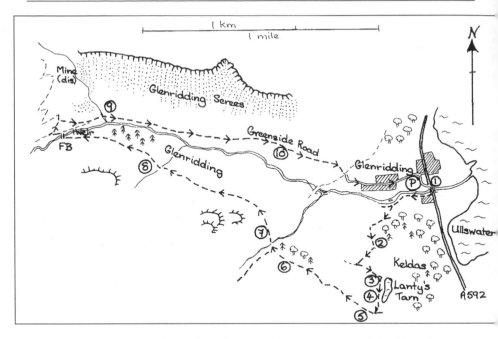

At the signpost turn left for Lanty's Tarn and Helvellyn to pass through deciduous woodland. At the next signpost take the left fork and begin the steady climb through alders.

☺ Alder leaves are dark green and heart-shaped. Both male and female flowers are found on the same tree. The male ones are the dangley catkins and the female ones the tiny more rigid catkins. Through the summer the female flowers develop into green 'cones' and in the autumn they become woody and black and stay on the tree. These will help you to identify the tree. Alder is often grown on ill-drained areas, their roots taking up much excess water. It makes poor firewood but yields good charcoal. It was used for the soles of clogs.

Alder

Q. Why do you think alders have been planted in this part of the wood?

A. A great deal of water flows down this steep hillside on its way to join the beck.

2. Continue climbing and then pause on the seat, with a good view of the lake. Go on through the kissing gate and walk ahead. Look over to the right, towards the head of the valley, to see your first glimpse of Greenside mine at the bottom of the steep sided Sheffield Pike. Ignore the gate ahead and turn sharp left to continue climbing more gently. As you go you walk on a pitched path.

☺ Pitching involves placing stones close together, upright, so that only the flat top edges show. The stones can extend downwards for as much as 2ft (0.6m). They are placed together like pieces of a jigsaw and little stones are added to fill gaps.

Q. Why do you think some of the paths are pitched?

A. To repair damage caused by the boots of walkers and by water coursing down these mountain paths.

3. Then the path levels and the tarn lies ahead. Before you continue you might wish to bear left and follow the track upwards to a small crag, Keldas, from where there is a wonderful view of Ullswater. About the little summit grow magnificent Scots pine, which provide a glorious frame to your photographs of the lake.

4. Return down from Keldas and pass through the gate to the side of Lanty's Tarn.

☺ In the days when it was used to provide ice for the Hall, the bottom of the tarn would be scrapped clear of weeds in the summer. In the winter, after the water had frozen, the blocks of ice would be cut. These were placed in an ice house nearby and covered with a lid. It was then packed with a layer of sawdust 3ft (0.9m) to 4ft (1.25m) thick to prevent warm air from melting the ice.

5. Walk on to the dam. Here turn right to take a narrow path leading across the fell. Watch out for the stile in the wall on the horizon, ignoring any paths that go off left or right. Pause here for another pleasing view of the lake.

6. Walk ahead along a glorious path, with the village of Glenridding below to the right. The way becomes indistinct for a short distance and then clear again as it descends gently towards the wall beside wood-

land on your right. Once clear of the trees the path joins another, becoming sturdily reinforced to cross a shallow ford over Mires Beck.

Q. Look right downstream. What do you think the wooden structure over the beck was used for?

Water wrack

A. Farmers in Lakeland call it a water wrack and it is used to stop farm animals and debris being washed downstream.

7.   **Stride on to ford another small stream and then, ignoring the stile on the right, bear left to walk beside the wall on your right.**

 As you go, look over the wall to see how man has influenced the landscape with walled pastures for his animals, the great tips of mine waste and the plantations of conifers.

 As you proceed you have a bird's eye view of the disused mine. Most of its remaining buildings have now been converted; one is an outdoor centre and the old stables have become the youth hostel. You can see traces of the supports of winding gear, but all the entrances have now been blocked.

 The Romans are believed to have worked the mine first. It was also worked in the 16th century, was at its most active in the first half of the 19th century, was electrified and modernised in 1903 and continued busily until 1962. It was one of the most successful lead mines in England. After the ore was smelted many thousands of tons of lead were obtained, plus a little silver. This operation resulted in the enormous mound of spoil which so disfigured this part of the dale.

8. **As you continue on the high-level path, children should be under close control. Continue to the bridge just above a weir, which is very spectacular when the beck is in flood. Cross and turn right to follow the waymarks through the buildings. As you go you can still visualise what it must have been like to work in such a hostile environment.**

☺ The mine is claimed to be 3,000ft at its deepest part. In 1959 it was used to test instruments for detecting underground atomic explosions.

Q. As you descend the reinforced track, look left to see small horizontal pieces of wood pegged into the scree of an old spoil heap. What do you think they were for?

A. These were used to help hold and colonise the scree with shrubs, grass and other plants.

Q. Does it look as if it has succeeded? If not why not?

A. The slope is too steep and the scree too unstable for vegetation to take hold.

9. **Continue on.**

☺ To your right Glenridding Beck hurries over its boulder-strewn bed. It was dammed in Keppel Cove to provide a head of water for the mine, but during a great storm in October 1927 the dam burst, sending a great flood of water down the valley, causing enormous damage. Miraculously, no human life was lost.

10. **Go on along the way where it becomes metalled and follow the road where it swings right and then left into the village. At the health centre, turn right to pass between the houses to return to the car park.**

Q. Look for the structure beside the information centre. Where did the containers come from and what are they carrying?

A. From the mine and they carry lumps of ore.

27. Aira Force, Lyulph's Tower, Ullswater

Lyulph's Tower, not open to the public, is a dramatic crenellated house built in 1782 by the Howard family, and was used in the 19th century by the Duke of Norfolk as a shooting lodge. It lies close to Ullswater and below the towering slopes of Gowbarrow Fell. It was built upon the site of an earlier tower and it is believed the name came from Ligulf, first baron of Greystoke. With the tower goes the romantic legend immortalised by William Wordsworth in his poem *The Somnambulist*. The legend tells of a beautiful damsel named Emma of Greystoke who was betrothed to an Arthurian knight, Sir Eglamore. He stayed away so long from his beloved, fighting evil, that he caused her distress and she took to sleep-walking. When he did return, in the middle of the night, he met fair Emma close to Aira Force. He touched her, she awoke and swooned over the edge. Sir Eglamore rescued her but she died in his arms. He became a hermit.

Starting point: The Aira Force National Trust pay and display car park on the A592 just east of the A5091. Grid reference 401201

By bus: See walk 26

Distance: 2 miles

Terrain: Easy walking but there are several drops about the falls and small children should be under control.

Map: OS Explorer OL5, The English Lakes – North Eastern area.

Public toilets: In car park

Refreshments: The Aira Force teashop a few yards from the car park. It is well signposted.

The Walk

1.   Start the walk by looking at the display boards before passing under the stone arch at the back of the car park.

Q. Who owns and looks after this part of the Lake District?

A. The National Trust.

2. **Go through the metal gate.**

Q. What can you see on the top of the gateposts of the metal gate?

A. An acorn, the symbol of the National Trust.

🙂 Pass through the next gate and beyond, lying on the ground, is an enormous tree trunk. Its hollow inside is large enough for a youngster to crawl through. Go on to a grassy glade surrounded by tall conifers, which have come from all over the world.

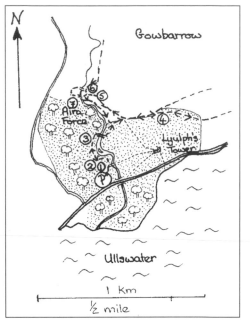

Q. What do you call the very tall tree over to your left with branches that curve upwards?

A. Monkey Puzzle tree, which originates from Chile.

3. **Cross a bridge and climb the steps, up and up, ignoring a left turn, and continue to take a stile on the right. Walk ahead to join a wider path and go on. Look right to see Lyulph's Tower. Stroll on for as far as you wish. The upper path pleasantly climbs the lower slopes of Gowbarrow Fell and gives good views, but very soon the ground drops away steeply to the right and it becomes vertiginous.**

🙂 In the 18th century Gowbarrow's slopes were home to 600 to 700 deer and gamekeepers were employed to keep predators at bay. The woodland of the lower slopes provided timber for bobbin and hoop making, bark for tannin and charcoal either for iron smelting or for making gunpowder. It was along the shores of Ullswater, below Gowbarrow, that Wordsworth walked with his sister Dorothy and was inspired to write the famous poem which begins:

I wander'd lonely as a cloud
That floats on high o'er vales and hills,
When all at once I saw a crowd,
A host of golden daffodils,
Beside the lake, beneath the trees
Fluttering and dancing in the breeze.

4. Return along the path and keep on the wider one to come to a gate back into the environs of Aira Force. Turn right and continue above the glorious tree-lined gill to stand on the bridge over the force. Take care here.

Q. What are the names of the men engraved on the plaque?

A. Stephen Edward and Gerald Spring-Rice.

Q. When did Gerald die and how?

A. 1916, fighting in the 1914-18 war.

5. Here you may wish to walk upstream. If so do not cross the bridge but go on to continue through oak woodland to see High Force, an impressive cascade that descends through a deep-sided chasm.

6. Return to the bridge with the plaque. Do not cross but descend the steps (rather steep for short legs), ignoring all other ways down into the gorge. Turn right and walk with care to stand on another bridge to view the high point of the walk.

☺ Here Aira Beck flows over the meeting place between Skiddaw Slates and the Borrowdale Volcanic series of rocks, the waterfalls cascading over shelves of the harder rock. Aira Force (force is Old Norse for waterfall) was visited in vast numbers by the Victorians, probably as many as today. If the beck is in spate be prepared to get damp as you view. Watch for rainbows as the sunlight, passing through the drops of water, is split into its seven colours.

7. Return from the bridge and remain on the path. Below, in the bottom of the gill, flows the beck, hurrying to reach the lake after its tempestuous fall. Enjoy the sheer beauty of the lovely gorge, much the same as it was when earlier generations came to view the magic of Aira. Follow the path back to the car park.

Aira Force

28. Hartsop

This walk visits the charming village of Hartsop. It continues along a path that climbs gently through natural woodland below Lingy Crags. From here you can look down on Brothers Water nestling in its hollow and enjoy a fine view of the valley northwards to Ullswater. After crossing Angletarn Beck you return by permissive paths alongside the Goldrill Beck and through more glorious woodland.

Starting point: Cow Bridge car park (it has two sections). Grid reference 403134 – the same as for the Brothers Water walk 29, with which this can be combined.

By bus: Kirkstone Rambler (517), limited service Bowness Pier to Glenridding. Stagecoach Cumberland. Inquiries 0870 608 2 608

Distance: 3 miles

Terrain: Easy walking but take care over slippery rocks and exposed tree roots after rain.

Map: OS Explorer OL5, The English Lakes – North Eastern area.

Public toilets: Glenridding

Refreshments: See walk 29

NB: The Hartsop walk and Brothers Water walk can be pleasingly joined.

The Walk

1.   From Cow Bridge car park, use the metalled footpath at the side of the A592, walking east in the direction of Kirkstone Pass. At the phone box continue on the same side of the road, following the signpost for Hartsop. Pass the Langton Adventure Centre on your left and go ahead.

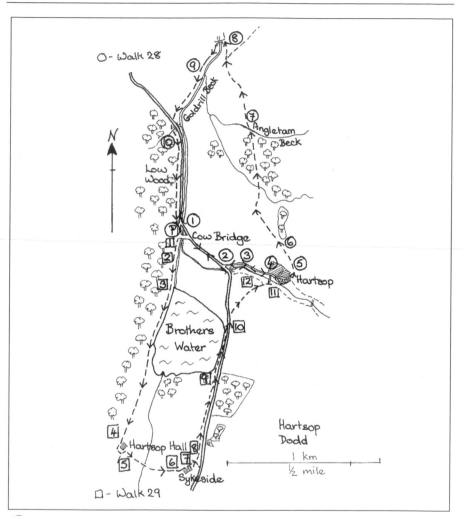

😊 Many Lakeland villages have grey stone houses like those that line both sides of the narrow lane. They were built with thick stone walls and slated roofs to keep out the heavy rain and the strong winds that can blow down the valley in the winter, and remain cool in the hot days of summer. Look over the field gate on the left to see a barn. It was once an early 18th-century drying kiln.

Q. What do you think was dried in the kiln and why?

A. Corn was dried. In the Lake District corn often had to be harvested while it was still wet.

'Spinning Gallery', Hartsop

2. **Walk on a few steps and look for several round chimneys on rooftops.**

Q. Can you suggest a reason for this shape?

A. Some say it is so that the devil cannot settle in a corner. Others that it was easier to build this way using local stone. It was certainly a traditional way of building in the Lake District.

3. **Continue slowly on.**

☺ See if you can spot some step-gabled roofs and suggest why they have such a name. There are two cottages with wooden spinning galleries. The name implies that here the occupants did their spinning but though some spinning did take place, they were used principally as passages between the upper rooms and also for storage.

4. **Walk on a few more yards to the signpost directing you left. Look about to see an iron door let into the wall at shoulder height.**

Q. What do you think it was used for?

A. It was an oven and dates from Victorian times.

5. **Turn left up the public footpath and pass through the gate to walk the concrete track. Look back to see more step gabling and a glorious view of the fells that surround Brothers Water (see walk 29). The path**

is well waymarked. Ignore any left or right turns. Notice the huge out-crops of rock as you go.

☺ As you walk look for large black birds, with heavy beaks, circling overhead. These are most likely to be ravens. Listen for their call as they fly – it sounds like a short deep bark. They nest on ledges on rocky outcrops, high on the crags.

Ravens

6. Go through the small gate onto the open fell and follow the narrow path that passes through scattered ash, rowan and sycamore. Avoid small wet areas and cross tiny streams by stepping on convenient stones. Then the path comes close beside a drystone wall. Pause again and enjoy the grand view. Climb the ladder-stile. Beyond, An-gle Tarn beck descends in many glorious waterfalls and cascades. If the level of the stream allows, cross it on boulders and descend through the bracken to the wide cart track, below on your left. If the beck is in spate, turn left and keep close to the wall to cross it by the footbridge lower down.

7. Go on along the track in the same general direction, with deciduous woodland over the wall to your left. Then, when the trees cease, you can look down on Goldrill Beck.

☺ This is the beck you saw at the car park. It flows out of Brothers Water and heads through flat land to Ullswater. After the last ice age much soil and debris, called alluvium, was washed down the mountain slopes. The beck carried it along and deposited it, in times of flood, in vast quantities between the two lakes, reducing the length of Ullswater.

8. Ignore the track that climbs right and go on to pass through a gate with a three-armed signpost beyond it. Turn acute left and walk on to cross the tractor bridge over the beck. Climb the stile immediately on the left. Stride along the alder-lined river now on your left.

☺ Alder likes rich soil and it cannot endure acidity or stagnant water; hence the reason for its thriving here. It has heart-shaped leaves and can be recognised by its black woody female cones. The tree is pollinated by wind and its tiny seeds have air bladders, which keep them afloat for dispersal by water. As you go look for the stones encased in tiers of metal cages that line the beck.

Q. What is their purpose?

A. Strong reinforcement for the riverbank when the Goldrill is in spate. They are placed where this part of the banking has been washed away in earlier storms.

9. Climb the stile and stroll along the narrow path, still with the beck to your left. Continue on to the stile to the A592. Take care here as you step down on to a sometimes busy road. Cross it to take the stile opposite.

10. Turn left to walk the permissive path that continues through pleasing woodland, above the road, and returns you to the car park. As you pass through the last gate notice the large stone that has been used to help the hinge do its job.

29. Brothers Water

This delightful small lake sits at the bottom of the Kirkstone Pass and south of Ullswater. Its regular shape makes it appear man-made but it is natural. Looking down from the surrounding mountains it is easy to imagine that it might once have been part of Ullswater. At its southern and northern ends there is flat land, providing some grazing for sheep The soil has been washed down from the slopes above, enriching the land, but farming is not easy in this area because of the extremes of climate. An average of 100 inches of rain falls annually.

Starting point: Cow Bridge car park (2 sections), both small. Grid reference 403134.

By bus: Kirkstone Rambler, limited service, Bowness Pier to Glenridding. Stagecoach Cumberland. Inquiries 0870 608 2 608.

Distance: 3 miles.

Terrain: Easy walking all the way. Take care with children as you cross the main road and as you walk it through the valley.

Map: OS Explorer OL5, The English Lakes – North Eastern area.

Public toilets: Glenridding.

Refreshments: At Syke Side farm shop.

Pushchairs: Terrain: suitable from car park to caravan site only, returning by the same route.

NB: The Brothers Water walk and Hartsop walk can be pleasingly joined. For map, see Hartsop Walk.

The Walk

1. **Pause by the large farm gate in the south-west corner of the parking area, on the west side of Goldrill Beck, to read the information panel.**

It has an excellent line drawing of the lake and the valley and gives much detail on the geology of the mountains. It explains that the present shape of the surrounding hills developed in the ice age when a large glacier carved out the characteristic shape of the valleys.

Q. What type of rock are the mountains composed of?

A. Volcanic rock.

Q. Before you set off look for the seat by the gate. What does the V stand for and what is the significance of the date?

A. V for Queen Victoria and in 1897 she celebrated her diamond jubilee.

2. Pass through the gate and look back to Cow Bridge.

Q. Has it been widened? How do you know? What might it once have been?

A. Yes. Look under the arch to see where the newer stucture joins the old. A packhorse bridge.

3. Continue beside the beck on your left, walking the wide track that edges oak and beech woodland. In spring and summer many wild flowers grow here and the trees are full of birdsong. Go on to pass the confluence of two becks and follow the track as it climbs gently above Brothers Water, believed to be so named after two brothers who drowned in it. Once beyond the trees look for birds on the lake.

☺ All year round you should see coot. These are small black ducks with white 'plates' above their white bills. Beyond the water's

Coot and water-lilies

edge is a wide area of rushes. Until the middle of the 19th century such plants were used to make rush-lights to illuminate houses. Their stalks were coated with animal fat.

4. **Pass through a kissing gate beside a farm gate. The mountain ahead is High Hartsop Dodd. Walk on to come to a fine working farm, named Hartsop Hall.**

☺ The present hall is about 400 years old. The original farm was built in the 12th century when the valley was part of a Norman hunting forest. In the 15th century the land passed to the Lowther family by marriage and became a farm and the house was rebuilt.

5. **Go through the next gate by the farm and follow the track as it swings left beyond the buildings. Use the gate beside the cattle grid to continue ahead.**

☺ Look ahead to see the sturdy wall built of rounded cobbles.

Q. Where do you think these cobbles came from and what do you think made them round?

A. The beck. The lively beck rubbed and pounded the boulders against each other. It rolled them along the bed of the stream, smoothing the edges and making them round.

6. **Cross the tractor bridge over the Kirkstone Beck.**

Q. What are the trees growing about the bridge?

A. Ash. The leaves are compound, with paired leaflets on either side of a mid-rib.

7. **Walk on to cross a gated cattle-grid.**

8. **Stroll on through Syke Side farm caravan and camping site. Ahead are the seemingly sheer slopes of Hartsop Dodd. At the branching of the way, take the left fork and continue almost to the road. Look for the wooden gate on the left. A notice tells you that this is a permissive path to Brothers Water, set up by the National Trust. Parents with pushchairs should turn back here.**

9. **Enjoy the lovely path, which eventually joins the road. It leaves it again after a couple of steps to descend though hazel scrub to the edge of the lake. Pass through the next kissing gate and go on. There are several small beaches here just made for picnics, if the lake is not too high.**

Q. What are the large leaves floating on the surface of the water?

A. Water-lilies. At the right time of the year they have large white flowers.

10. Stroll the path to a gate onto the main road. Cross with care and take the signposted walled cart track that continues in the same general direction. Look for the holly growing close to the wall. It thrives in unpolluted air. Cross the small clapper bridge.

Q. What has been used to build it?

A. Two large slabs of slate.

11. Follow the way to the narrow road that passes between the lovely old houses of Hartsop village. Spend some time looking for rounded chimneys, spinning galleries and step gabling (see walk 28). If combining walks 28 and 29, turn right here. To return to the car park, turn left.

12. Walk the lane to where it joins the main road. Remain on the right side, using the pavement, to return to the car park.

30. Howtown to Glenridding

This seven-miler starts with an exciting trip on an Ullswater ferry from Glenridding, across the lake to Howtown. The walk back along the footpath, which is clear to follow, is considered by many people as the most delightful in Lakeland. The two steamers, MY *Raven* and MY *Lady of the Lake*, are two 19th-century 'steamers' now converted to oil cruising. Perhaps you will travel on the Raven, which was built near Glasgow and transported in sections by rail to Penrith and then by horse dray to Pooley Bridge, where it was assembled. The Lady of the Lake was launched in 1877. Ullswater is 7½ miles long and runs from Glenridding in the heart of the mountains to Pooley Bridge, where the River Eamont flows out of the lake.

Starting point:	The car park at the pier, Glenridding. Grid reference 390169. For the walk Howtown pier grid reference 444198.
By bus:	Stagecoach Cumberland, Ullswater Rambler 34 from Workington via Keswick. The Patterdale Bus 108 (Sundays only). Inquiries 0870 608 2 608.
By car:	Glenridding is on the A592 at the southern end of Ullswater. Pooley Bridge is 5 miles from M6, junction 40, Penrith.
Distance:	7 miles with no escape route. Five-year-olds have been known to walk it but it is more suitable for older children.
Terrain:	Distinct path or track, with several ups and downs. Occasionally rough under foot.
Map:	OS Explorer OL5, The English Lakes – North Eastern area.
Public toilets:	At start of approach road to pier. On both steamers.
Refreshments:	Glenridding, Patterdale, Pooley Bridge, hot drinks on boats. Ullswater Steamers, Inquiries 017684 82229.

Head of Ullswater

The Walk

☺ In 1927 a great storm raged (see walk 26) and the dam on the beck above Glenridding, provided for use by the lead mines, burst. The debris washed down the valley formed the stony peninsula over which you walk or drive to reach the pier.

☺ If you can stop looking at the glorious views and leave your seat on the steamer you might wish to find the answers to the following questions. Any of the crew who are not busy might help you.

Q. What is the age of the boat you are on and how many people does it carry?

A. Look for the answers on a prominently displayed plaque.

Q. How many red and white life-belts can you see?

A. Eight on 'Raven' and six on 'Lady of the Lake'.

Q. How many flags can you see and what are they?

A. 'Raven' carries two and 'Lady of the Lake', three. The red triangular flag is the flag of the company owning the boats. The white triangular flag is a pilot flag. The red flag with the union jack in the corner is nicknamed the red duster.

Q. What is the flag on the pier?

A. The union jack, or union flag.

☺ As you travel along the lake, look right to glimpse the footpath along which you will return. Watch for the tall waterfall, Scalehow Force; you pass below this but have a better full length view from the steamer.

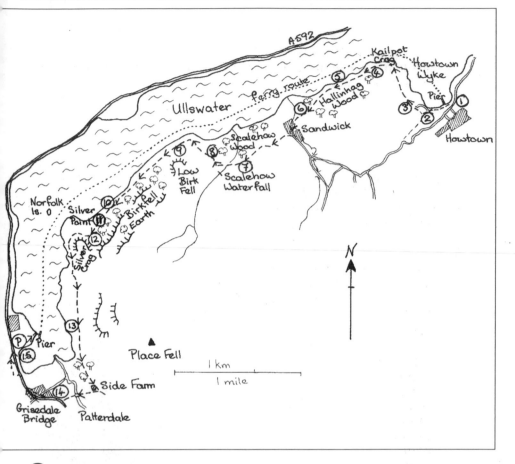

☺ If you are among the last to leave the boat you could find out how the crew manage to bring it in sideways to the pier. This pier too is constructed on debris washed down by a beck – the Fusedale Beck, which you cross almost immediately.

1. Walk along the railed pier and cross the footbridge on the right, following the signpost directions for Sandwick. Stride on the pleasant path from where you might see the steamer making its return trip or continuing on to Pooley Bridge.

2. At the next signpost follow the directions for Patterdale. Climb the steps.

Q. How many are there, if you include the stone at the bottom?

A. 28

3. **Turn right to walk the level path, from where there is a glorious view. Look to the foot of the lake to see Dunmallard Hill (walk 31). Above you is Hallin Fell.**

Q. What is the date on the seat on this footpath?

A. 1931-1988

4. **Continue on the path over Kailpot Crag and then the pleasingly pitched way through the oaks of Hallinhag Wood. Look for rowan, Scots pine and some glorious beeches. Go on near to the shore and walk with care over the exposed tree roots. The boulders on the woodland floor are heavily cloaked with mosses and lichens.**

Q. What birds would be likely to nest here and why?

A. Pied flycatchers, tree creepers, greater spotted woodpecker, great and blue tits. They make use of the abundant holes and crevices in the bark of the mature trees.

🙂 Look for the ferns growing up from the moss-covered higher branches of the ancient oaks. These are epiphytes. They use the tree for support, so that they obtain more light and air than if they grew on the woodland floor. They do not obtain nourishment from the tree.

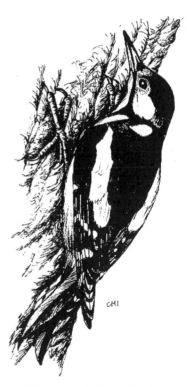

5. **Follow the path as it descends towards a kissing gate near the shore. Beyond is a delightful shingle reach of the lake. Pass through the kissing gate on your left and then go on through two more gates. Turn left to walk beneath a row of fine larches and beside Sandwick Beck. Cross the hurrying stream by a wooden bridge into the hamlet of Sandwick.**

6. **Turn left to walk the metalled road and right again beyond Townhead**

Greater Spotted Woodpecker

Cottage, the last building on the right. Climb a steep rough track. Then the way levels out and continues beside a wall and a fence to your right.

☺ Notice to your left, just before and after Sandwick, that the hills are smooth and round. As you go on you will notice that they become rough and craggy. This difference is caused by the underlying rock. Under the more gentle rounded slopes is found a type of rock known as Skiddaw Slate and the rougher craggy rock is Borrowdale volcanic.

7. **Pass a delightful barn with a pleasing porch. Then go on to cross the bridge over the Scalehow Beck, just the place for a paddle.**

☺ Above is the waterfall seen from the boat. The beck tumbles over the fault where the Skiddaw Slate and Borrowdale Volcanic rocks meet.

8. **Follow the rough path as it climbs and then goes on up beside a wall, beyond which is Scalehow Wood. You have another view of the waterfall from here. Then the path continues high above the lake, with scattered birches below and hawthorn above the path. Look for juniper bushes as you stroll on.**

☺ Juniper berries, a favourite with coal tits, are used to flavour gin. Hams were once cured in juniper smoke. Best quality gunpowder was manufactured using charcoal obtained from juniper bushes. Superstitious folk in times gone by thought that juniper would protect them from witchcraft.

☺ Look across the lake to see Lyulph's Tower, a hunting lodge built in the 19th century (seen on walk 27), and the woods about Aira Force, visited on the same walk. It was on the lake shore near these two that Wordsworth saw the daffodils that inspired his poem, which tells of a 'host of golden daffodils'.

9. **Continue to Long Crag, a high point with a dramatic view. Then as you descend towards the lake you pass through scree slopes, where birches thrive.**

Q. How do the trees help to stabilise the scree?
A. Their long trailing roots weave between the rocks.

10. **Go on down the path through the scattered birch, juniper and rowans on the slopes below Birk Fell Earth.**

☺ Look out for your first view of House Holme Island (Norfolk Island on the OS map). Here you can usually see cormorants holding out their wings, as if to dry. It is believed that this stance helps them to digest their food.

11. **And then the trees cease and you cross a small beck that issues from Silver Crag. Stroll on along the clear way, with the attractive Silver Bay and its beach to your right, just before Silver Point. The many small paths continuing out to the rocky promontory reveal its popularity.**

12. **Saunter on as the path winds round below Silver Crag and as it continues uphill towards a walled way through woodland.**

☺ Look for very high wire fencing, on the left, around some of the trees.

Q. Why do think it is twice as high as that normally used?

A. It is deer fencing and deer can jump very high. They like to eat the bark of trees.

13. **Go on past a step gabled barn and a huge oak tree and then continue to Side farm, where you turn right for Glenridding, as directed by a signpost. Stroll the wide track through pastures to cross Goldrill Beck (seen on walk 29). At the road, cross and turn right. Pass St Patrick's church. The pavement runs out here so cross the road again. This area is known as The Butts, where archery was practised and the stocks stood.**

14. **Continue on and take the permitted path through trees when the pavement runs out again. At the end of this path, cross the road with care, to take another permitted path that goes on through trees, above the road. This returns you to the road. Cross it, again with care, to go through a gate in the fence. Stride the track, past a small snack bar, and with the lake to your right.**

☺ Notice the trees planted along the edges of the track. Each has a metal label below it.

Q. What countries are named and what is the event commemorated?

A. You might spot Denmark, Greece, Ireland and Germany. They were planted to mark the formation of the single European market in 1992.

15. **The track returns you to the car park and the pier.**

31. Dacre and Dalemain, Pooley Bridge, Ullswater

This is a most pleasing walk, starting from Dunmallard Hill, Pooley Bridge, and going on to Dacre Church and Dacre Castle. It continues on a wide track through quiet pastures to Dalemain, a stately home with an animal garden and agricultural museum. The return is made over rolling pastures and then beside the River Eamont.
It is a walk that all the family will enjoy, with clear footpaths and tracks, from which you will see much bird and animal life.

Starting point: The National Park's Dunmallard pay-and-display car park, on the west side of the Eamont and the village of Pooley Bridge. Grid reference 469245

By bus: Stagecoach Cumberland, Patterdale bus 108 (Sundays only), Penrith, Pooley Bridge, Patterdale. Inquiries 0870 608 2 608

Distance: 5 miles

Terrain: Easy walking. Short steepish climb at the start. Two very short stretches of the A592 cannot be avoided.

Map: OS Explorer OL5, The English Lakes – North Eastern area.

Public toilets: In the village

Refreshments: In Pooley village and at Dalemain

The Walk

1. **Walk back to the entrance of the car park on the B5320 and take the kissing gate on the right to follow the track leading right, signposted Dacre. Climb the wide way which, initially, ascends below an arch of trees.**

🙂 To your left rear up the steep tree-clad slopes of Dunmallard Hill,

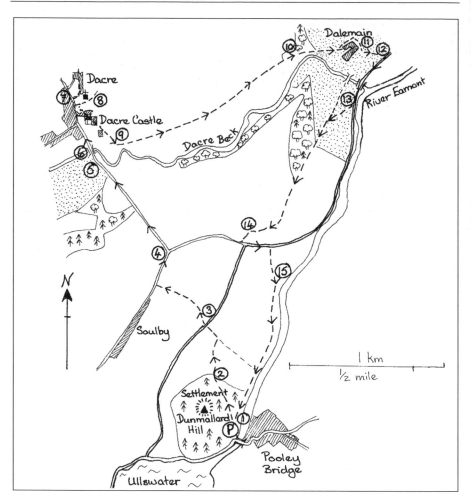

a prominent landmark at the northern end of Ullswater. On the summit are traces of an iron-age fort.

2.   At the three-armed signpost, leave the woodland and pass through a gate on the right. Stride across the pasture, bearing slightly left to a stile with a white-topped post beside it. Go on in the same general direction to the next stile, which is heavily laden with arrows and signs. Beyond, turn left and descend by the wall to a stile to the A592, which you cross with care.

3.   Go through the kissing gate opposite and walk ahead, following the signposted way (directions on pieces of slate). Climb the stile over a

wall into a very narrow lane. Turn right and walk to the T-junction, where you turn left.

Q. Beyond the parish notice board, what species of tree is protected by a wooden enclosure?

A. An oak.

Q. What does it commemorate?

A. The centenary of Dacre parish council, 1894-1994.

4. **Use the wide green verge to walk towards Dacre.**

Q. What do the letters stand for on the seat at the side of the road?

A. Queen Elizabeth II.

Q. What is the significance of the date 1953?

A. The year of the Queen's coronation.

5. **Then you come beside a grassy area by Dacre Beck.**

☺ In spring the banks of the beck are covered with snowdrops. From here you can see the rounded hump of Little Mell Fell, an outlier of the Helvellyn range.

6. **Cross the single arched bridge over the beck and stroll on to the centre of the village and its delightful green.**

Q. What do you think the iron rod attached to a post in the middle of the grass was used for?

A. It is not, as you might suppose, the remains of stocks, but the support for a road barrier made of poles and used long ago.

7. **Beyond the telephone box, turn right and walk up the little hill to the parish church of St Andrew. Go inside and enjoy the lovely church, parts of which date from Norman times (13th century).**

Q. The clerestory windows are those high up above the nave. Are they all the same shape?

A. Some are arched and some are rectangular.

Q. Are the pillars all the same shape?

A. Some are round but most are octagonal.

Q. Why do you think the bible in a glass case is chained to the wall?

A. It dates from 1617 when bibles were rare and valuable and they were chained to prevent their being stolen.

☺ The chancel is an early part of the church and possibly dates from the 12th century. The communion rail is late 17th or early 18th century. Beyond the rail and to the left (in the Sanctuary) is a medieval effigy in red sandstone of a cross-legged knight. It is thought to be a crusader, possibly a Lord Dacre. Also in the chancel are two fragments of a cross and on a display stand is a 9th century fragment, with intricate carvings on it. Can you make out what they are?

☺ Outside in the churchyard are carvings of four bears. They are believed to be medieval and maybe they tell a story. Can you find all four and imagine what sort of story they illustrate?

Stone bear, Dacre

8. **Leave by the gate in the south wall, bear right and follow the track round left to Dacre Castle.**

☺ The striking 14th-century sandstone Dacre Castle is a pele tower. It is 66ft (20m) high. It provided protection for the villagers and their stock against marauders from over the border. William de Dacre, who died in 1319, is believed to have built the castle. In 1307 he was allowed to crenellate, or fortify, his house. In 1354 Margaret de Dacre created a chapel in the castle. Today it belongs to the Hasell family, who live at Dalemain. It is not open to the public.

9. **Continue along the cart track, with the castle to your right. The way passes through large fields with deep soil. Those on the right lead down to the beck. To the left of the track are many newly planted trees in protective wooden 'cages'. Further on look for a fine avenue of trees bordering the track. Oak trees alternate with poplars.**

☺ The poplars in this avenue are growing to an immense height. Notice that all the branches follow the upward trend of the main trunk. Poplars demand rich soil with abundant moving water.

Q. Do they have these two essentials?

A. Yes. You can see that the soil is good, with few stones, and a small beck hurries along close to their roots.

10. **Follow the track to the outbuildings of Dalemain. Look left over a gate as you go, from where you can often see fallow deer.**

Q. How can you tell the stags (males) from the hinds?

A. The males have antlers.

11. **Follow the track as it bears round right into a large cobbled court-yard.**

☺ The courtyard is part of Dalemain, an attractive house with a fine Georgian facade. The estate was bought in 1679 by Sir Edward Hasell. Parts of the house are probably 15th or early 16th century. The house and gardens are open to the public and in the courtyard is a board detailing the cost of entry. There is also a gift shop, restaurant and two museums. One displays old agricultural machinery and is to be found on the upper floor of the huge barn overlooking the courtyard. There is no fee for entry. In the garden is an animal garden, where children will enjoy looking at many plants all of which have an animal in their name, e.g. snapdragons, cow parsley, elephants ears, monkey flower, goat rue, hawkweed, goatsbeard and more. Adults have to pay to visit the gardens but some age groups of children go free.

12. **Follow the track, leaving the courtyard on your left. Continue towards the A592, by a track that swings sharp left. Beyond the gate, turn right, and using the grass verge walk with care along the A-road, where you have a good view of the Georgian front to the house. Cross the road bridge over Dacre Beck and take the signposted footpath on the right.**

13. **Walk diagonally uphill, following short white-topped posts, to come to the side of a wood and then a stile. Beyond, walk on along the stiled way, with a good view of the Lakeland mountains ahead.**

☺ Keep a look out here for hares. They have a longer body, longer back legs and longer ears than rabbits. In March male hares often do seem mad, like the one in "Alice in Wonderland". They race after each other at great speed, oblivious of human presence. They kick each other, grunt, and occasionally have stand-up boxing matches.

14. **Follow the track as it drops down to a stile to the right of a clump of trees. Walk across a narrow pasture to a sturdy stepped stile to the**

Hares boxing

A-road again. Turn left and walk with care. Well before the corner, and again with great care, cross the road to take a signposted kissing gate. Cross several footbridges and walk on to take a stile on the left. Beyond this is a small tarn, where you can sometimes see oyster catchers.

☺ Oyster catchers are nicknamed 'sea-pies'. They have long sturdy orange bills, fleshy legs and black and white plumage.

15. Follow the track by the fence on the right. Walk on bearing right, with the wide fast flowing River Eamont away to your left. From now on the way is sheer joy, first beside the river and then through trees close to the Eamont to return to the car park.

☺ The River Eamont flows out of Ullswater and passes below the 16th-century bridge at the end of the car park.

Q. How many arches does it have?

A. Three.

Q. How many cutwaters does it have and what are they?

A. Four. Cutwaters, shaped like the prow of a boat, are to be found at water level on the outside of the arches supporting the bridge. They break the flow of the river before it reaches the supports, in this way reducing the force on the masonry.

32. Small Water and Blea Water, Haweswater

These two lovely tarns are found high up above Haweswater in corries overshadowed by Harter Fell, Mardale Ill Bell and High Street. This circular walk climbs first the easy but steepish rocky staircase to Small Water. It continues over grassy slopes, winds round rocky outcrops and skirts a boggy area. One more short climb brings you to the austere Blea Water. The return to the shores of Haweswater is by a long grassy path.

This is an adventurous and exciting walk for youngsters. If the circular walk is too arduous both tarns could be visited seoarately and the return made by the outward route.

Starting point: The free car park at the head of Haweswater, approached by the road from Shap via Bampton Grange and Bampton Bridge, passing the great dam and then traversing the east side of the reservoir. Grid reference 469108

By bus: No public transport Stagecoach Cumberland to Shap village only. Inquiries 0870 608 2 608

Distance: 3½ miles

Terrain: A clear rocky path to Small Water. Indistinct grassy trods, followed by a climb up to Blea Water. Long grassy descent.

Map: OS Explorer OL5, The English Lakes – North Eastern area.

Public toilets: Shap car park

Refreshments: Shap village

The Walk

1. **Walk ahead from the car park to pass through a kissing gate and on to the signpost with white arms.**

Q. What does MCWW stand for on the signpost?

A. Manchester Corporation Water Works.

2.   Walk ahead, ignoring paths and tracks off left and right, in the direction of Kentmere. Cross a small beck and go on along the good track. The looming wall of sheer crags to the left is Harter Fell. Pause at the kissing gate and look back on the way you have come and down onto the reservoir.

☺ Haweswater reservoir supplies water for Manchester. Before construction of the dam in 1929 Hawes Water was a silvery tarn reflecting the firs and fells of the valley. Beyond, towards the head of the valley, stood Mardale village, which once had a little church with yew trees, a fine Hall, the Dun Bull inn, bridges, walls, flowers, hedges and farms. All these were covered as the water rose.

☺ Sometimes you can see a bleached area around the shoreline, where more water has been drawn off than has been replaced by rainfall.

Q.   After a prolonged drought what do you think happens?

A.   The level of the water falls so low, drawn off by thirsty Manchester, that the ruins of the drowned village are exposed.

3.   Walk on to cross the beck on large boulders and then on to the brow ahead, from where you have a superb view of waterfalls and becks that tumble out of Small Water and Blea Water. Pass through the next gate and go up. Cross another small stream on a slab of slate.

☺ About the main stream, Small Water Beck, ash and rowan grow .

Slate slab bridge

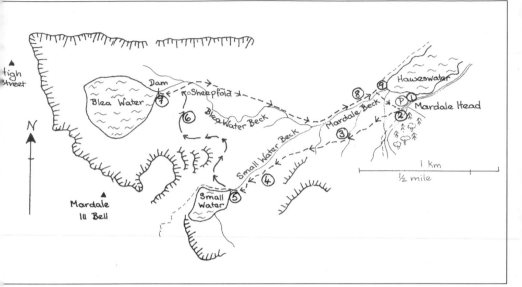

Q. What is the other name by which rowan is known?

A. Mountain Ash.

4. **Go on up a great mound of moraine, material carried and dumped by a retreating glacier during the ice-age, to come to the side of the pleasing Small Water Tarn, the place for your first stop.**

☺ The tarn sits in a steep-sided corrie where glacial ice

Rowan

ground out a circular hollow. The mound you just climbed blocked the water from leaving except for where the beck emerges. In parts it is 52 feet (15m) deep.

5.   Cross the outlet by stepping stones, walk on a few yards and then ascend the grassy slope to your right. Go on, leaving a small tarn away to your right. Avoid the wettish areas and then move over to below the steep slopes to your left, walking below the scree skirt. Descend a grassy slope. It also is wet after rain, so hug the bottom of the scree. Wind round the bottom of the spur. Do not descend to the boggy bottom, but keep up the easy grassy slopes, aiming for a buttressed trod ahead and a sheepfold clearly seen to your right.

Q.   Who do you think made the buttressed way and where do you think they lived?

A.   Quarry workers, who might have lived at Mardale.

6.   Wind round to pass above the sheepfold and continue on a narrow trod to the side of Blea Water Beck. The footbridge is a ruin and you will have to step across the narrow hurrying water at a convenient place. Once across, walk ahead to join a clear path, where you turn left. The path gets lost in the mire only once. Go on up beside the beck to come to the edge of the magnificent corrie tarn.

☺ This is a much larger tarn, with sheer sides which descend almost perpendicularly into the water. It is believed to be over 200 feet (61m) deep in parts. It is often in shade and the reflections in the water are sombre and austere.

7.   Leave by the path you used to reach the tarn. Do not cross the beck, but continue on the clear path parallel with it. It stretches ahead of you over grassy slopes. The grass-coloured humps about you are more glacial moraine. Avoid the wet areas and continue on the lovely way. Climb the ladder-stile beside a gate. As you descend look across right to see the silvery becks and waterfalls seen earlier from the other side of the valley.

8.   Go on down and, just before the next stile, look right to see Dodderwick Force The long plume of white water sends up clouds of spray which tangles with the birches hanging overhead.

9.   Beyond the stile turn right to cross several footbridges to return to the parking area.

33. The Rigg, Haweswater

This is a short walk for the younger members of the family. It takes you along the head of the reservoir and then climbs the path to the fir trees on The Rigg, a rocky promontory projecting into the lake. Keep a look-out for a very large bird because you are in the territory of England's only golden eagles. The pair return each year and nest in the mountains close to Haweswater. To find food for their young they need to search regularly, flying over a vast area. The reservoir is inhabited by schelly fish, a relic from the ice-age. Several groups of people have teamed up to try to save it from extinction. Numbers of this rare fish are in decline because of the fluctuation in the level of the reservoir (see walk 32).

Golden Eagle

The differing levels disturb the areas of grass and silt on the shore where the schelly lay their eggs. To combat this problem artificial grass beds have been installed underwater and weighted down at a depth of 9½ft (3m). It is hoped this will provide safe areas for the eggs to hatch and develop into young fish. Some of the eggs will also be removed to Blea Water and Small Water (see walk 32).

Starting point: See walk 32

By bus: See walk 32

Distance: 1½ miles

Terrain: Rocky path, pleasingly pitched in places. Short sharp descent to the side of the lake. Long climb up a shadowy ride below Norway spruce. Return by the same rocky path.

Map: OS Explorer OL5, The English Lakes – North eEstern area.

Refreshments and toilets: See walk 32

The Walk

1. Walk ahead from the car park to pass through a kissing gate. Go on to a three-armed signpost. Turn right to walk in the direction for Bampton. Cross several footbridges and then bear right round the corner of the reservoir.

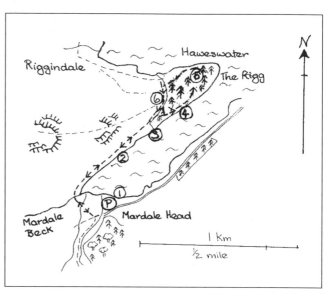

🙂 Notice the sturdy wall to your right. Drystone walls were built with no mortar to hold the stones together, as in a brick wall. Each stone was selected to fill a space in the best way possible. In this wall you can see that some very large field boulders have been used at the foot. On the top is a neat row of 'cams'. These discourage sheep from jumping over and they also put pressure on the stones below, adding to stability. They often protrude towards the next farmer's land.

2. **Continue on the steadily rising rocky path.**

🙂 To the left are scattered straggly hawthorns. They are not very tall, they lean and they are rather wizened.

Q. Can you suggest why they are not like hawthorns found in hedgerows?

A. They are battered by the wind on the exposed slopes of Dudderwick The nutrients, and the soil, are washed away down the slopes by heavy rainfall.

🙂 Look over the wall as you climb higher to see more dilapidated walls that run to the water's edge and others that continue under water.

Q. Can you suggest why?

A. These are the walls of farms that were submerged when the valley was flooded.

3. At the edge of the conifers, look for the stile into the trees. There is a steep step down on the far side which young children might need some help to negotiate. Descend the short steep slope and then continue along the narrow shore path. If the water level is low this will present no problem. If the lake is high you may prefer to move into the trees and continue.

4. After 200 yards (183m) a wide track ascends steadily. This passes below Norway spruce and the way underfoot is deep in needles and soft to walk.

☺ Norway spruce is the well known Christmas tree. The cones are long and curving and are a glossy light brown colour, much favoured by squirrels.

5. Continue to the top of the slope, where tall larch trees grow.

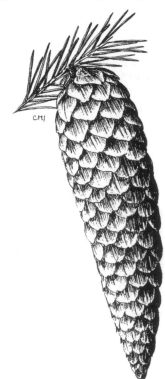

Q. What is different about the woodland floor here compared with that below the spruce trees?

A. Grass and moss grow in profusion, encouraged by the extra light they receive. Larch loses its leaves in winter and the foliage in summer is much less dense than that of other conifers.

6. A similar stile to the one crossed to enter the trees stands on the edge of the woodland. Take this to rejoin the path. Turn left and begin your descent. At the head of the reservoir turn left, cross the footbridges and then turn left again to regain the car park.

Norway Spruce cone

34. Keld Chapel and Shap Abbey

This splendid short walk from Shap village takes you through the wide rolling countryside of the eastern edge of the National Park. From it there are dramatic views of the Lakeland mountains and of fine pastures, edged with limestone walls, that lie between the village and the Mardale fells. The solid houses of Shap lie on either side of the A6, the village standing about half-way between Penrith and Kendal. In 1763 the first stagecoach made the perilous journey over Shap fell, when the turnpike road was built from Kendal to Eamont Bridge. At either end of the village you can see the steps used by weary stagecoach passengers to alight.

The turnpike road became the A6. Until 1971, this main north to south trunk road along the north-west of England carried an enormous amount of traffic through the village. In winter this bleak and wild route is often blocked with snow. Lorry and car drivers would become trapped in the village, or on Shap Fell, until the snow plough could get through to clear the road. Shap villagers earned a great reputation for giving freely of food and shelter to travellers stranded in bad weather and a memorial plaque, set in a pillar of slate on the highest part of the road, pays tribute to this generosity.

Today, with the construction of the motorway (M6) through the Lune Gorge, well away from the village, Shap has become a much quieter place. You can cross the road in safety.

Starting point: Shap Memorial Park car park on the east side of the main street. Grid reference 564151

By bus: Stagecoach Cumberland. Infrequent service from Penrith, bus 106/107. Inquiries 0870 608 2 608

Distance: 4 miles

Terrain: Easy walking on footpaths over pastures. Many stiles to be climbed – these are stone-stepped and well built, making them easy for all to climb and descend.

Map: OS Explorer OL5, The English Lakes – North Eastern area.

Public toilets: In car park

Refreshments: In the village

The Walk

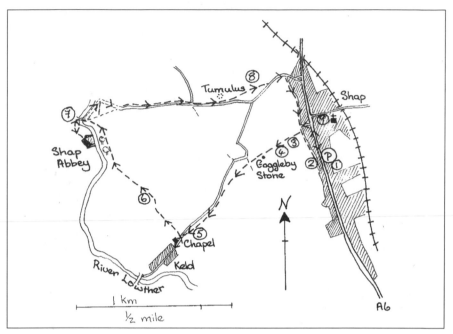

1. **Return to the entrance of the car park.**

Q. When was the Memorial Park opened and why?
A. 1951 for the Festival of Britain.

Q. Whom did it commemorate?
A. The people who died in the 1939-45 war.

2. **Cross the road and walk right to look at the market cross, which houses Shap library. The arches have been filled in and windows added.**

Q. When was the charter for a market granted?
A. 1687

3. **Walk on until you reach the fire station. Turn left into West Close and take the first left. The footpath to Keld is signposted on the right. Pass through a gate to walk a long narrow grassy pasture between walls to go through the next gate. Continue gently uphill and wait for the**

magic moment when the Lakeland fells come into view. Notice also the delightful patchwork of limestone walls.

4. Go through the next two gap stiles and then walk over to the Goggleby Stone, a standing stone, thought to have been placed there in Neolithic times. Stride on to a gap stile, cross a track and another stile. Beyond bear slightly left to come to a wall edging the road. Here turn left and follow it to climb the next stile. Stroll on past a gate to take a stile through the wall to join the narrow road. Walk left towards the hamlet of Keld, which stands on the banks of the River Lowther. The first building on the left is Keld Chapel.

Goggleby Stone, Shap

☺ The chapel is thought to have been built, in the 16th century, by the monks of Shap Abbey. In the 18th century it was used as a cottage and a chimney was built. Today it belongs to, and is cared for, by the National Trust.

Q. Where does the notice on the door suggest you obtain the key?

A. At the house opposite.

☺ Go inside the tiny building. It still has some of the original windows.

5. Leave the chapel and return uphill to take the signposted gate in front of the last house on the left. Move over to the wall on the right and walk ahead to the stile. Beyond, stroll on. Where the wall turns away right, continue ahead, soon to walk beside another wall on your left. Watch out for the easy-to-miss stile over the high wall on your left.

Q. How many steps do you take to climb up and how many to come down the other side?

A. Nine on both sides.

6. Continue beside the same wall, now on your right, heading for some trees. Climb the stile to the left of a gate and saunter on, with the trees and a wall to your left. Watch for your first glimpse of the abbey, in its hollow on the left. Continue ahead to the road. Turn left and descend the concrete track to the side of the River Lowther. Do not cross the bridge but turn right as directed. In the trees, close to the river you might see a red squirrel. Cross the footbridge over the Lowther and follow the track that leads to the kissing gate into the grounds around the ruins.

☺ The abbey stands in a glorious sheltered hollow, with the River Lowther flowing close beside it. On a sunny day the stones have a pinkish tinge. In this idyllic corner you might be tempted to picnic on one of the seats. The abbey was founded in the 12th century by Thomas Gospatric. It was dissolved in 1540. All that remains is the impressive west tower of the abbey church, built about 1500. There are many smaller fragments of 13th- and 14th-century buildings. See if you can discern the outlines of the church from these.

Q. To whom is the abbey dedicated?

A. St Mary.

Shap Abbey

Q. Which canons founded the abbey?
A. The white canons.

Q. Why were they called this?
A. They wore white robes.

7. Retrace your steps over the footbridge and climb up the concrete track, continuing past a house on the left. Go on ascending to a gate across the road. Take a stile in the wall to the left of the gate. Beyond, stroll the large pasture, with the wall to your right to a stile in the far corner. This gives access to a road. Cross this and take the signposted gate opposite and saunter on with the wall to your right.

☺ Just before the next stile is a grassy knoll on your left, marked as a tumulus on the map, which means that it might be an ancient burial mound.

☺ Look at the walls as you go. Some have huge boulders, probably cleared from the fields and used as footings. Most drystone walls are really two walls, filled in with rubble and then tied together with large flat stones, called throughs.

Q. How many rows of throughs can you see in the walls you are walking beside?
A. Two. These are sturdy walls. Some walls are built with no throughs and are not so strong.

8. Walk on to the wall ahead, cutting off a curve in the wall on the right. Emerge from the pasture by a signposted gate on the right. Continue on along the road for 100 yards (91m) to take a signposted grassy track on the right side of the road. This leads you, behind the houses of the village, to West Close, where you turn left to rejoin the main road. Cross and walk right.

☺ To visit the attractive parish church, turn left. St Michael's is attractively set among trees It has a pleasing tower under which you pass to enter the church. The south chapel has a barrel roof.

9. Return to the main road and walk on to rejoin your car.

SOUTH LAKELAND WALKS WITH CHILDREN
Nick Lambert

The companion guide for complete coverage – children really can enjoy walking with the help of Nick Lambert's guide. He seems to have thought of everything to keep both parents and children happy – clear directions take you along 20 varied, well-maintained paths which can be tackled by even the youngest family members. **£6.95**

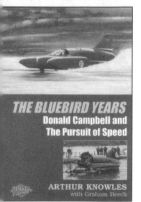

THE CONISTON TIGERS: Seventy Years of Mountain Adventure
A. Harry Griffin

Lakeland Book of The Year, 2000! The life story of A. Harry Griffin MBE, Country Diary writer for *The Guardian*. "A very special book . . . a living history of Modern Lakeland climbing" – Chris Bonington. **£9.95**

IN SEARCH OF SWALLOWS & AMAZONS
Roger Wardale

This is a revised edition of a popular book originally published in 1986. Additional material has been added to satisfy even the most avid reader of "Swallows & Amazons" – three decades of Ransome hunting with text and photographs to identify the locations of the ever-popular series of books. **£7.95**

THE BLUEBIRD YEARS: Donald Campbell and the Pursuit of Speed
Arthur Knowles with Graham Beech

Fully revised account of Donald Campbell's attempts to raise the world water-speed record in "Bluebird" to 300mph. Includes recovery of the wreck and the funeral of Donald Campbell in 2001. "It's a damn good read and there are plenty of rare photos." – *Focus magazine* **£9.95**

BEST PUB WALKS IN THE LAKE DISTRICT
Neil Coates

This, the longest-established (and best-researched) pub walks book for the Lakes, is amazingly wide-ranging, with an emphasis on quality of walks and the real ale rewards that follow! **£6.95**

BEST PUB WALKS ON THE LAKELAND FRINGES
Neil Coates

In this collection of 25 walks, Neil Coates urges ramblers to discover the tranquillity of the mountain paths, wild woodland, waterfalls and local heritage of the Lake District fringes. Walks range from 4 to 11 miles and each one features a refreshing stop at a quiet village pub or country inn, personally selected by the author. **£6.95**

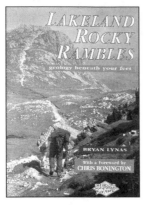

LAKELAND ROCKY RAMBLES: Geology Beneath Your Feet
Bryan Lynas
This is the perfect way to learn about why things look the way they do in our most beautiful National Parks. "Refreshing ... Ambitious ... Informative ... Inspiring" – *New Scientist*. **£9.95**

100 LAKE DISTRICT WALKS
Gordon Brown
If you plan to buy just one book of Lakeland walks, this is the one you need: "A useful addition to any walker's library" – *West Cumberland Gazette*. **£7.95**

LAKELAND CHURCH WALKS
Peter Donaghy and John Laidler
Nominated for Lakeland Book of The Year, 2002 – and with a foreword by Simon Jenkins of *The Times*. 30 detailed circular walks ranging from 3½ to 12 miles with alternative shorter options, each starting from a noteworthy church. **£8.95**

MORE TEA SHOP WALKS IN THE LAKE DISTRICT
Norman and June Buckley
Leisurely rambles in fine scenery with the bonus of afternoon tea or morning coffee – or both – in a variety of tea shops from tiny cafés to stately homes. Crossing both the central regions and the lesser-known fringe areas, their 25 easy-going, circular walks range from 2 to 9 miles. **£6.95**

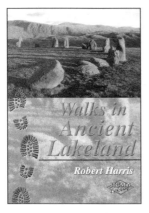

WALKS IN ANCIENT LAKELAND
Robert Harris
A collection of circular walks ranging in length from 2 to 10 miles, each visiting sites and monuments from the Neolithic and Bronze ages, linked where possible with ancient trackways. All walks are accompanied by sketch maps, and the author's intricate hand-drawn sketches. **£6.95**

WALKING THE WAINWRIGHTS
Stuart Marshall
This ground-breaking book is a scheme of walks linking all the 214 peaks in the late Alfred Wainwright's seven-volume Pictorial Guide to The Lakeland Fells. After an introduction to the Lake District, the route descriptions are clearly presented with the two-colour sketch maps facing the descriptive text – so that the book can be carried flat in a standard map case. The walks average 12 miles in length but the more demanding ones are presented both as one-day and two-day excursions. "An excellent, concise manual on how to tackle the 'Wainwrights' in an intelligent way" – A Harry Griffin MBE. **£7.95**

All of our books are available from your local bookshop. In case of difficulty, or to obtain our complete catalogue, please contact:
SIGMA LEISURE, 5 ALTON ROAD, WILMSLOW, CHESHIRE SK9 5DY
Phone/Fax: 01625-531035 E-mail: info@sigmapress.co.uk
For the latest news and a browsable updated, catalogue, visit us on the World Wide Web
– **www.sigmapress.co.uk**